THE GARDEN OF EDEN

Books by Adam Pfeffer

Published by iUniverse:

KOLAK OF THE WEREBEASTS

TWILIGHT OF THE GODS

THE MISSING LINK

TO CHANGE THE WORLD and OTHER STORIES

THE DAY THE DREAM CAME TRUE and OTHER POEMS

THE VISITORS

THE CREATION OF GOD

THE AMAZING SLICK MCKINLEY:
GREATEST ATHLETE EVER

THE FANTASTIC FLYING MAN

THE GENIUS WITH THE 225 IQ

30 GREAT STORIES FOR OUR CENTURY

WILD TALES

HAMMERIN' HANK GREENBERG:
THE JEWISH BABE RUTH

THE GARDEN OF EDEN

THE
GARDEN
OF
EDEN

A PLAY IN THREE ACTS

ADAM PFEFFER

iUniverse, Inc.
Bloomington

The Garden of Eden
A Play in Three Acts

iUniverse books may be ordered through booksellers or by contacting:

iUniverse
1663 Liberty Drive
Bloomington, IN 47403
www.iuniverse.com
1-800-Authors (1-800-288-4677)

ISBN: 978-1-4759-7706-6 (sc)
ISBN: 978-1-4759-7707-3 (e)

Printed in the United States of America

iUniverse rev. date: 02/14/2013

Cast of Characters

GOD

ADAM

THE SERPENT

EVE

CAIN

ABEL

ACLIMA

AWAN

VOICES FROM ABOVE

SETH

Act One

A man, Adam, is sitting beside a river in a nude body suit as God, an old man in a gray beard wearing a flowing white robe and holding a staff, stands beside him in the place known as, The Garden of Eden. The garden is filled with all kinds of bushes and vegetation and exactly two trees.

GOD: Are you happy now?

ADAM: Happy? What do I have to be happy about?

GOD: Fruit and good, clean water.

ADAM: You call that happiness?

GOD: But I have made it for you.

ADAM: And you made me from the dirt—

GOD: From the dust of the earth.

ADAM: I'm nothing but a bunch of dirt.

GOD: You are a man.

ADAM: A man, a man, nothing but dirt.

GOD: But there is water.

ADAM: If I jump in the water, I'll be nothing but mud.

GOD: You are a man.

ADAM: And what the hell am I supposed to do with myself?

GOD: Enjoy yourself.

ADAM: By myself?

GOD: Oh, but of course, you need companionship.

ADAM: I need something more than fruit and water.

GOD: I will make you companions.

ADAM: Yes, anything is better than fruit and water.

GOD: Quite interesting. I was going to call this place, paradise.

ADAM: I was going to call it boring as hell.

GOD: One man's paradise is another man's hell. I must remember that.

GOD walks off into the distance and disappears from the stage. ADAM is left alone sitting by the river.

ADAM: He calls this place paradise?

A SERPENT, the size of a man, walks up to ADAM and grins.

SERPENT: Enjoying yourself?

ADAM: Who the hell are you?

SERPENT: A neighbor, you might say.

ADAM: A neighbor? Well, that makes sense.

SERPENT: What do you mean?

ADAM: Ah, you can always tell what kind of neighborhood it is by the neighbors who live there.

SERPENT: And what exactly does that mean?

ADAM: You're not the sharpest knife around, are you?

SERPENT: But you mock me.

ADAM: Now you're getting the hang of it.

SERPENT: But, sir, you haven't even given me a chance.

ADAM: You don't deserve one.

SERPENT: But, you see, I know this place very well.

ADAM: That's not much.

SERPENT: But look at those trees, my friend.

ADAM: That's the best you can do?

SERPENT: Those trees are very important.

ADAM: The hell with them.

SERPENT: No, you don't understand.

ADAM: No, you don't understand if you think those stupid trees are so exciting.

SERPENT: But look at them.

ADAM: Yeah, they look just great.

SERPENT: Do you know anything about them?

ADAM: Do I care?

SERPENT: Oh, you would care if you knew something about those trees.

ADAM: I can't believe I'm having a conversation about trees.

SERPENT: Now listen Buster Brown—

ADAM: Who the hell is that?

SERPENT: Never mind, you just think about those trees.

ADAM: The trees again? Isn't there anything else about this place that gives you some enjoyment?

SERPENT: You don't understand, you fool.

ADAM: I'm the fool?

There are suddenly footsteps off-stage.

SERPENT: Dammit, here comes that foolish Lord again.

ADAM: You call everybody a fool and you're the one excited about some trees.

SERPENT: Well, can't stay, I'll be seeing you later, neighbor.

ADAM: I'll count the moments.

The SERPENT sneaks off. There is whistling and then GOD appears from off-stage.

GOD: Adam, I have brought you a companion.

A goat appears from behind GOD.

ADAM: Are you insane?

GOD: But it is a thing I made for you.

ADAM: You're wackier than that other guy who was here talking about the trees.

GOD: What do you call it? I want you to name everything.

ADAM: I call you a boob.

GOD: But the goat can be your companion.

ADAM: Thanks a lot, but I had something a little more arousing in mind.

GOD: Oh, I see. How about a lion?

ADAM: No, I don't think so, Lordy.

GOD: But I am making all of these things I call, animals, for you.

ADAM: Animals don't really send me. Get my meaning, you old codger?

GOD: But I put a hump on the camel—

ADAM: Hump, that's it!

GOD: You want the camel?

ADAM: No, I want the hump.

GOD: And a camel will not satisfy this need?

ADAM: You are an old pervert, aren't you?

GOD: What about a lamb?

ADAM: No, I need something softer.

GOD: But the lamb is quite soft.

ADAM: No, softer skin and a softer voice.

GOD: I was afraid of that.

ADAM: What?

GOD: Afraid of what you're talking about.

ADAM: You know what I mean?

GOD: Oh, I know all right.

ADAM: Well, can you do it?

GOD: You sure you know what you're getting yourself into?

ADAM: It's got to be better than a camel or a lamb—

GOD: (*pausing*) I don't know about that.

ADAM: But I don't want an animal.

GOD: I was afraid of that.

ADAM: Then you'll do it?

GOD: I guess I have no choice.

ADAM: I hope you know what you're doing.

GOD: I hope so, too, for the sake of all of us.

ADAM: Gee, it can't be that bad, can it?

GOD: You'll have to give a rib for me to do it.

ADAM: What? A rib?

GOD: Only way I can do it.

ADAM: But a rib?

GOD: Oh, stop being a baby.

ADAM: But is it worth a rib?

GOD: (*pausing again*) Good question, but I guess it has to be done.

ADAM: But a rib?

GOD: Oh, it will be over before you know it, I guess.

ADAM: What do you mean, I guess?

GOD: You'll see. God help us all.

ADAM: But you're God.

GOD: I know, alas, I know. (*shaking his head*).

ADAM: What do I have to do?

GOD: Nothing but provide a rib.

ADAM: That's all?

GOD: For now, my son, for now.

ADAM lies down on the ground and GOD stands over him with his arms raised. Curtain closes.

Scene II

GOD: Wake up, Adam.

ADAM: Is it over?

GOD: Just beginning, my son.

ADAM: You took the rib?

GOD: And I made something for you from the rib.

ADAM: Good, let's see.

GOD: I hope you're not disappointed.

ADAM: What is it?

GOD: I call it a woman.

ADAM: A woman?

GOD: It's much like you.

ADAM: (*frowning*) How much?

GOD: You'll see.

From behind GOD appears EVE, a voluptuous woman in a nude body suit with brown hair and a beautiful figure.

ADAM: Holy cow!

GOD: Now control yourself, my son.

EVE: Hi boys, are you excited to see me?

ADAM: Don't you know it!

EVE: You look pretty slick, hon, won't you give a lady a hand?

ADAM: You betcha.

GOD: Now be careful, my boy, keep your mind sharp.

EVE: Oh, there's no need for him to do any heavy lifting any longer.

GOD: That's what I was afraid of.

EVE: You just let Eve do the thinking about how to make this place some sort of home.

ADAM: Yes, dear.

GOD: He learns quickly, I'll give him that.

EVE: There are a few changes we have to make around here.

ADAM: Gee, but He calls it paradise.

EVE: I bet he does.

GOD: But I made everything to your satisfaction.

EVE: That's what you say, darling.

ADAM: But it's paradise.

EVE: To me it's a dirty pig sty.

GOD: I knew it (*shaking his head*).

EVE: What are all those things walking around?

GOD: I call them animals.

EVE: Takes one to know one.

GOD: Now see here.

EVE: This place is so unsanitary.

ADAM: Yes, unsanitary.

GOD: I've lost him already.

EVE: You've got those things called animals just doing what they please as we try to live with some sort of dignity.

ADAM: Yes, dear.

GOD: I know I didn't touch his spine.

EVE: You just leave everything to Evey and this place will be somewhat livable eventually.

GOD: I knew I was making a mistake.

EVE: Mistake? I'll tell you what was a mistake. Having a river flowing right through the front yard.

GOD: Fruit and water is all one needs.

EVE: A typical male.

GOD: Now see here, sweetheart, you're not really one to tell me my business.

EVE: Your business? And don't call me, sweetheart.

GOD: How should I address you?

EVE: Ms. Eve, if you don't mind.

ADAM: Ms. Eve, you want me to get rid of Him?

EVE: No, that's all right, darling.

GOD: Ms. Eve, for heaven's sake.

EVE: I'm just going to do a little straightening up if you don't mind.

GOD: Fine, I made it for you and him. (*He looks at ADAM and shakes his head*).

EVE: And we'll quite enjoy it after a few changes are made.

GOD: If it pleases you.

ADAM: Yes, dear. You sure you don't want me to throw Him out?

EVE: No, it's quite all right, furry face.

GOD: Furry face?

EVE: Now look at all this fruit lying around.

GOD: Be careful.

EVE: What do you mean?

GOD: I mean I want you to stay away from those trees.

EVE: Is there something wrong with them?

GOD: Just stay away from them.

EVE: You're going to have to do better than that, sweetie. If something's not right around here, I want to know about it.

GOD: Well, that tree over there with the apples is the Tree of Knowledge of Good and Evil. You don't want to have anything to do with that one.

EVE: But the apples are pretty.

GOD: Pretty? You stay away from those apples. They're nothing but trouble.

EVE: But they look good for my complexion.

GOD: They'll make you ugly as sin.

EVE: What about the other tree?

GOD: That's the Tree of Life. You stay away from that one, too.

EVE: Then what are we supposed to eat around here?

GOD: Oh, there are other things to eat. I provided a veritable feast for you.

EVE: But no apples.

GOD: No apples.

EVE: How about if we just pick them off the ground?

GOD: No apples.

EVE: But they look so delicious.

GOD: They're bitter inside.

ADAM: But if you didn't want us to eat them why did you make them in the first place?

GOD: I have my reasons. You just see that you don't eat them. I'm warning you.

ADAM: And what if we eat them, anyway?

GOD: (*thinking*) I won't let you be together.

ADAM: What?

GOD: That's right, Adam. I won't let you see Eve anymore.

EVE: Oh, don't let Him scare you, hon.

GOD: You better watch your step, Ms. Eve, I can unmake you, too.

EVE: Pig.

GOD: You just behave yourself.

EVE: I know my rights.

GOD: What rights?

EVE: The rights of a free woman.

GOD: Free woman. You just stay away from those trees.

ADAM: I don't need those stupid apples, anyway. They're for a woman.

EVE: What? Oh, I see I'm going to have to teach you a thing or two.

ADAM: You teach me?

EVE: Something your mother should have done.

ADAM: Mother? But we have no mother. (*pointing at GOD*) Just him.

GOD: I'm your father and mother. You listen to me.

EVE: I'm going to have so much to say to my analyst when he's created.

GOD: You just stay away from those apples and those trees. Now I have to go and create another galaxy. You both better behave.

EVE: Oh, we'll behave all right.

ADAM: (*smiling*) I'd rather be a little naughty if you know what I mean.

EVE: (*smiling*) Oh, you're so bad, sweetie.

GOD: Just make sure you stay away from those apples.

(GOD *exits*)

ADAM: You want to go for a swim?

EVE: No, hon, that's all right, you go.

ADAM: It will put you in the mood.

EVE: The mood, hon? Oh, Adam, you are an animal.

ADAM: Softer than a goat.

EVE: Is one of those dirty things walking around here?

ADAM: They won't bother you.

EVE: Good, now you go and take that swim.

ADAM: All right, scaredy cat, I'll look forward to seeing you very soon.

EVE: Yes, hon, very soon. (*watches as ADAM walks off*) Now I'll see about those trees.

EVE walks to the two trees and begins looking around. There are apples on the ground and she picks one up. The SERPENT appears from behind one of the trees. The size of a man he walks up to EVE with a smile on his face.

SERPENT: Afternoon, ma'am.

EVE: Afternoon yourself.

SERPENT: Admiring the fruit?

EVE: Is it yours?

SERPENT: No, I just live here like you.

EVE: You were created, too?

SERPENT: You could say that.

EVE: You like God?

SERPENT: Oh, he's okay.

EVE: Does He tell you what to do?

SERPENT: No, I like to think I have a free will to do as I please. What about you?

EVE: Yes, I guess so.

SERPENT: Bet he told you not to eat those apples.

EVE: Wrong, dear, He said He made everything for us.

SERPENT: Sure is a nice apple. Don't you think so?

EVE: (*pausing*) Apples, apples, doesn't anybody around here think about more than just eating all the time?

SERPENT: He told you not to eat the apples, didn't he?

EVE: He might have mentioned it.

SERPENT: You're not scared of Him, are you?

EVE: Scared of God? Of course not.

SERPENT: Then eat the apple.

EVE: And why do you care so much?

SERPENT: Just think it's the right thing to do if one considers themselves a free person to do as they wish.

EVE: You know something about those apples?

SERPENT: They're the most delicious items in this entire place.

EVE: How do you know? Have you eaten them?

SERPENT: Of course I've eaten them.

EVE: Even if God said to stay away from them?

SERPENT: Oh, He doesn't tell me what to do.

EVE: I guess not. You're free to do whatever you like.

SERPENT: That's right, missy.

EVE: Then let me see you eat one of those apples right now.

SERPENT: Certainly.

The SERPENT picks up one of the apples and then hears a noise off in the distance. He puts down the apple.

SERPENT: Maybe another time, missy, I'm expected somewhere just about now.

EVE: I bet you are. You're scared of Him, aren't you?

SERPENT: I didn't even know He was coming.

EVE: I bet you creep.

SERPENT: Now, now, let's not insult each other.

EVE: I want to see you eat that apple right in front of God.

SERPENT: Maybe another time, sugar.

EVE: Don't you sugar me.

SERPENT: Well, I'll be seeing you again.

EVE: Coward.

SERPENT: Now let's be reasonable, dear.

EVE: Oh, go on if you have to.

SERPENT: I'll come back and show you how good those apples are. Promise.

EVE: Pig!

The SERPENT hurries off leaving EVE standing near the two trees. She hears footsteps and then starts to leave.

GOD: Didn't I tell you to stay away from those trees?

EVE: I just came to look.

GOD: Look, but don't touch. Understand?

EVE: But what's so special about those trees?

GOD: I really shouldn't have made them. They're poisonous.

EVE: Poisonous?

GOD: Yes, sugar plum.

EVE: But one of the neighbors said they've eaten them.

GOD: What neighbors?

EVE: Why that's what he said he was.

GOD: Who have you been talking to?

EVE: Oh, it doesn't matter.

GOD: Just don't believe everything you hear, dearie.

EVE: But you made everything.

GOD: Yes, but there are good days and there are bad days.

EVE: You don't know everything you've created?

GOD: Not getting any younger, you know.

EVE: But surely you're aware—

GOD: Just stay away from the apples.

EVE: But if they're so bad why did you make them?

GOD: Good question, my dear.

EVE: And the answer?

GOD: I was inspired.

EVE: That's your answer?

GOD: Where's Adam?

EVE: He's swimming in the river.

GOD: Good, clean water. That's all one needs.

GOD walks off into the distance.

EVE: Pig!

ADAM: (*in the distance*) Eve! Eve!

EVE: Pig!

ADAM: (*coming closer*) Eve, where are you?

EVE: Right here, darling.

ADAM: What are you doing here?

EVE: Oh, so you're afraid, too?

ADAM: Afraid of what?

EVE: Afraid of Him?

ADAM: You're seeing someone else! I knew it!

EVE: I'm talking about God, you idiot.

ADAM: Oh, Him. I'm not afraid of anyone or anything.

EVE: Yes, my dear, I believe you.

ADAM: Why is He bothering you?

EVE: Relax, He-Man, I was just coming here to look at the apples.

ADAM: Apples? But God said not to.

EVE: And do you think we should listen to everything He decides to tell us?

ADAM: Well, He did create everything around here.

EVE: Including us.

ADAM: Including us.

EVE: Then if we're His creations and the apples are His creations, we should be able to eat them if we want to, right?

ADAM: I don't know, he was pretty adamant about not eating those apples.

EVE: But they're only apples.

ADAM: But He said not to.

EVE: Do you love me, Adam?

ADAM: Sure I love you, sugar pie.

EVE: Sugar pie? Never mind. Well, if you love me, then you want me to be happy. Right?

ADAM: Sure, honeybunch.

EVE: Then if you love me and want me to be happy, then you'll eat the apples.

ADAM: But God said not to.

EVE: (losing her cool) God said not to, but I said I want to.

ADAM: I don't know, babe, I don't want anything screwing up our living situation.

EVE: Oh, there are plenty of places to settle down.

ADAM: But He calls this paradise.

EVE: Paradise, some paradise.

ADAM: But we have everything we need right here, love.

EVE: That's right and if I want to eat the apples, I will.

ADAM: Why do you need the apples? There are so many other things to eat.

EVE: But I want the apples.

ADAM: I'll talk to Him about it, dear.

EVE: Men are always talking about what to do. I want someone to do something.

ADAM: Let me smooth things over. You'll have your apples.

EVE: Promise?

ADAM: I'll promise if you give me a kiss.

EVE: Okay, one little kiss.

EVE kisses ADAM on the lips.

ADAM: Holy cow!

EVE: You liked that?

ADAM: And how.

EVE: There are more where that came from.

ADAM: What do you mean?

EVE: I mean, get me those apples and I'll give you more kisses.

ADAM: Oh, boy, that's a deal!

There's a noise off-stage and then GOD appears once again.

GOD: What have you been doing?

EVE: None of your business.

ADAM: That's telling him.

GOD: Didn't I tell you to stay away from those trees?

ADAM: We can go anywhere we like, isn't that right, Eve?

GOD: Oh, so now our Adam has a backbone, is that it?

EVE: You got it, chief.

GOD: At least you know who's running this show.

ADAM: Who is?

GOD: I am, Hercules.

ADAM: He is.

EVE: And what if we say we're free.

ADAM: Yeah.

GOD: You're as free as I say you are, got it?

EVE: Men. All a bunch of pigs.

GOD: Now Eve, you stop that. Adam and I love you very much.

EVE: How much?

GOD: As much as you want.

EVE: As much as letting us eat the apples?

GOD: No one's eating those apples. I told you.

ADAM: But Eve thinks we have a right to eat those apples.

GOD: Oh, Eve thinks, does she? Well, good for her.

EVE: I just think that if you made those apples and you made us, why not let us enjoy what you have made?

GOD: Oh, no, you don't want to start with me, darling.

ADAM: But give us a good reason at least.

GOD: You want a good reason? I'll give you one. The day you eat one of those apples from the Tree of Knowledge of Good and Evil you shall surely die.

EVE: And what does that mean?

ADAM: Yeah, what does that mean, you old geezer?

GOD: You don't understand. You're both still young and are enjoying the peace and serenity of a paradise.

ADAM: How can a little apple change all that?

GOD: These apples are not to be fooled with. They contain some powerful agents that I was not aware of at the time I created them.

EVE: How about if we take a little bite? Just to sample them. Just to see.

GOD: No, I forbid it. You have a nice life here. You have each other now and you have all of this that I have created. You love her and, in time, she will love you just as much in return. You have a good, happy life together in a paradise if you don't throw it all away on some poisonous apples.

EVE: But how will we know if we don't experience it for ourselves?

GOD: This time, you have to take my word for it.

ADAM: But we're free.

GOD: And you'll stay free a whole lot longer if you listen to me. Do you love her, Adam?

ADAM: More than anything in the world, Lord. She is the bones of my bones, flesh of my flesh.

GOD: Then why do you want to go and ruin it?

ADAM: Eating those apples will ruin it?

GOD: That's what I'm trying to tell you. Those apples are evil little things I had no business creating.

ADAM: Well, I really don't need them.

GOD: That's good, Adam, and what about Eve?

EVE: They probably have little worms in them, anyway.

GOD; Yes, right, my lovely Eve.

ADAM: Is that all that's bothering you, big guy?

GOD: Everything else is yours to enjoy.

EVE: Oh, great, even the goats?

GOD: The goats are very valuable, my darling, and they provide food and companionship.

EVE: I have nothing to say to a goat.

ADAM: What about me, dear?

EVE: You're softer than a goat.

ADAM: *(smiling)* Yes, that's true.

GOD: And what about me, sweetie?

EVE: You're just an old goat.

GOD: Right, my Evey. Now that we straightened out this business about eating the apples, I have some very important business to attend to. You enjoy yourselves in this beautiful paradise.

GOD exits.

EVE: Beautiful paradise. I still say it's aching for a woman's touch.

ADAM: I'm going to go for a swim.

EVE: Yes, you do that, my darling.

ADAM: You don't want to come along?

EVE: I would love to, but there's something I have to do.

ADAM: Okay, but the water feels great.

EVE: I think I'll join you later, my darling.

ADAM exits. EVE immediately hurries off to the two trees and bends down and picks up an apple. The SERPENT enters with a smile.

SERPENT: Lovely fruit, wouldn't you say?

EVE: How would you know?

SERPENT: Oh, I eat those apples all the time.

EVE: Even if He says not to?

SERPENT: He doesn't control me. I am free to do as I like.

EVE: And you know something about these apples?

SERPENT: You know it, missy.

EVE: Well, what's so special about them, anyway?

SERPENT: These apples, my little lady, will make you think things you never thought before in your wildest dreams.

EVE: *(getting excited)* What kinds of things?

SERPENT: Why once you eat these apples, you'll be wiser than any beast of the field.

EVE: Who cares about being wiser than a silly old goat?

SERPENT: It is said "the fruit of the tree in the midst of the garden" will make you equal to a God.

EVE: But He said we will die if we eat the apples.

SERPENT: But you will not die.

EVE: No?

SERPENT: No, you see He doesn't want you to eat the apples because if you did, you would be as wise as Him, knowing good and evil.

EVE: Good and evil? Hmmm, I thought so.

SERPENT: Yes, He doesn't want you to be as powerful and knowledgeable as He is.

EVE: Yes, that's what I thought.

SERPENT: Why you would be a God!

EVE: A God!

SERPENT: Now do you understand why those apples are so important?

EVE: *(excited)* I would be a God.

SERPENT: Yes, dearie, you would be as powerful as Him. Think of it. You would be the most powerful female in the universe.

EVE: Oh, the things I would be able to do. The universe needs a woman's touch. That old goat shouldn't be the only one who does creating around here. It needs a woman.

SERPENT: You're starting to understand.

EVE: A chance to finally have a say on how things are done around here.

SERPENT: Yes, you would be able to do anything you wanted.

EVE: Anything.

SERPENT: And you would know everything you needed to know.

EVE: Everything.

SERPENT: And you would be above everybody.

EVE: Everybody.

SERPENT: All you have to do is take a bite out of one of these apples.

EVE: A bite.

SERPENT: A nice, big bite.

EVE: A big bite.

SERPENT: Yes, little darling, all you do is bite into one of these apples and your troubles are over.

EVE: It sounds so easy.

SERPENT: And it is, my dear.

EVE: Just a bite.

SERPENT: Well, after the first bite, you'll want to eat as many of them as you can.

EVE: Yes, bite the apple.

SERPENT: Bite the apple, hon.

EVE: And He'll never know.

SERPENT: I won't tell Him.

EVE: How will He ever find out?

SERPENT: Not from me, I can tell you that.

EVE: And Adam won't tell Him.

SERPENT: Not if you get him to eat the apples, too.

EVE: *(smiling)* Yes, Adam will eat the apples, too.

SERPENT: And you both will be like Gods.

EVE: Yes, like Gods.

SERPENT: Why not try it?

EVE: *(holding an apple in her hand)* I'll take a little bite.

SERPENT: No harm can come from that, my dear.

EVE: A little bite.

SERPENT: Eat it.

EVE: *(bringing the apple closer to her mouth)* Yes, they are very pretty.

SERPENT: Eat it, my dear.

EVE: *(closing her eyes and opening her mouth)* One little bite can't hurt.

SERPENT: Eat it!

EVE: *(taking a bite)* It's so good.

SERPENT: *(laughing)* Yes, yes, eat it, my dear.

EVE: *(swallowing)* Oh, my goodness, but I feel weird.

SERPENT: Yes, yes, eat the apple!

EVE: Oh, maybe I shouldn't have.

SERPENT: No regrets, my child, keep eating.

EVE: *(eating the apple)* I feel smarter already.

SERPENT: Yes, I told you how wise you would be.

EVE: *(finishing the apple)* Did you know there are about 100 billion stars in our galaxy alone?

SERPENT: *(smiling)* Yes, you ate the apple, my dear, and now you will be a God.

EVE: Shooting stars are not stars but meteorites. They are particles from space entering and burning up in the earth's atmosphere.

SERPENT: Yes, very impressive, my dear.

EVE: There are ten different types of clouds.

SERPENT: Yes, very interesting.

EVE: Cirrocumulus, cirrostratus, altocumulus...

SERPENT: Happy, Doc and Dopey.

They suddenly hear ADAM calling from off-stage. He is trying to find EVE.

EVE: Oh, good, it's Adam.

SERPENT: Now remember you want him to eat an apple, too.

EVE: Yes, of course, an apple.

ADAM: Eve, are you all right?

EVE: Adam, darling, I'm so glad you found me.

ADAM: You are?

EVE: Yes, of course.

SERPENT: Hello, neighbor.

ADAM: What is he doing here?

EVE: He's a friend, Adam, darling.

SERPENT: Yes, I'm here to make you a God.

ADAM: A God? What is he talking about?

EVE: Oh, Adam. *(holding an apple).*

ADAM: But God said not to.

EVE: Are you going to listen to Him or me?

ADAM: But He created us.

EVE: And I'll give you something even better.

ADAM: What's that?

EVE: Oh, I can think of something (*putting her hands on him*).

ADAM: You ate one of them, didn't you?

EVE: You mean *Malus domestica*?

ADAM: No, I mean one of these apples.

EVE: That's what I was talking about. You see Adam, those apples make you wise until you're equal to a God.

ADAM: Who told you that? Him? *(pointing at the SERPENT).*

EVE: What difference does it make? All you have to do is eat the apple and you will be able to tell God what to do.

ADAM: I don't know, Eve, we're not supposed to do that.

EVE: Why? Because He tells you? Well, I say I've had enough being told what to do by Him. These little apples can change all that.

ADAM: But how do you know?

EVE: Look at me, darling (she bends down and picks up one of the apples).

ADAM: I think we should go, Eve.

EVE: Go? But I'm just starting.

ADAM: (looking at the SERPENT) It was you, wasn't it? You put all those ridiculous ideas in her head.

SERPENT: They're not ridiculous, my friend.

ADAM: Since when I'm I a friend of the likes of you?

SERPENT: I'm only trying to help both of you.

ADAM: Help? Yeah, right.

SERPENT: You don't understand how powerful these apples are.

ADAM: Yeah, but He said not to.

SERPENT: Because He's afraid, my son.

ADAM: Afraid? What does He have to be afraid of?

SERPENT: The both of you.

ADAM: But He created us.

SERPENT: Yes, but these apples from these two trees can make you as powerful as He is. Just one bite and you'll begin to see the truth.

ADAM: I don't know, He said not to fool around with these apples.

SERPENT: Don't you want to be as powerful as a God?

EVE: Well, I know I do *(she bites into the apple)*.

ADAM: Eve!

He watches her chew the apple and then swallow it.

EVE: The pomaceous fruit of the apple tree.

ADAM: The apple made you say that?

EVE: It makes you smart, Adam.

ADAM: It does?

EVE: Yes, just one bite and you'll understand.

ADAM: Like He understands?

EVE: Yes, just like Him.

ADAM: But what if He finds out?

EVE: I won't tell him.

SERPENT: And I surely won't tell him.

ADAM: Well, okay, the animals won't tell him, either.

EVE: No, He won't find out, my darling.

SERPENT: *(getting excited)* Eat the apple, my son.

EVE: You won't regret it, I promise you.

ADAM: And it makes you wise?

EVE: As smart as Him, my darling. We can rule together the whole universe.

ADAM: Just you and me, honeybunch?

EVE: Just you and me, my darling. He won't be able to tell us what to do anymore. We'll be able to do whatever we want.

ADAM: Yes, and you'll be my queen.

EVE: And you'll be my king.

SERPENT: Eat the apple, my boy, and you'll understand everything.

EVE: Yes, take a bite, my darling.

ADAM: A bite?

EVE: Yes, just one bite and you'll understand.

EVE places one of the apples in ADAM'S hand.

SERPENT: Take a bite.

ADAM: It's so red and beautiful.

EVE: Yes, it is, my darling. And they're very delicious.

SERPENT: Take a bite.

EVE: Yes, why don't you take a bite, dear?

ADAM: *(hesitating and staring at the apple)* I'll just take a little bite and see how I feel.

EVE: Yes, do it.

SERPENT: Take a bite.

ADAM: What harm can there be in one little bite?

EVE: Yes, you'll feel so much better.

SERPENT: You'll be a God.

EVE: A God, Adam, don't you understand?

ADAM: *(mesmerized)* A God.

ADAM brings the apple closer to his mouth.

SERPENT: Take a bite. There's no harm in that.

EVE: Yes, my darling, bite into the apple and be my king!

ADAM: A God, a king!

ADAM opens his mouth.

SERPENT: Bite into it and feel the power, my boy.

EVE: My king.

ADAM: King of the universe!

SERPENT: Yes, all will obey. Take a bite.

EVE: A God, my king.

ADAM bites into the apple and the SERPENT begins to laugh. It is a hideous laugh that echoes through the garden.

ADAM: *(holding the apple that now has a bite mark)* Oh, no, what have I done?

The SERPENT continues to laugh.

SERPENT: I'll tell you what you have done. You have eaten of the forbidden fruit!

ADAM: *(dropping the apple)* Oh, no, now I understand. Good and evil and wisdom.

EVE: But He will never know, my darling.

ADAM: We will hide from him.

EVE: Hide?

ADAM: Oh, my goodness, we have to hide from each other now.

EVE: I feel so ashamed.

SERPENT: *(laughing)* Because the both of you are naked!

ADAM: Naked.

EVE: Naked. Oh, I really have to put something on, my darling.

ADAM: So now we're beginning to become cognizant of right and wrong.

SERPENT: Don't you feel something else?

ADAM: An urge of some kind.

SERPENT: Yes, an urge to make love to her.

EVE: Oh, Adam, I feel it, too.

ADAM: Oh, we have surely sinned.

EVE: And we will sin again.

SERPENT: Yes, now you understand the power and wisdom of the gods.

ADAM: What will He say when He finds out?

EVE: Oh, who cares? I love the power and freedom of the knowledge we've obtained.

ADAM: It is quite liberating.

EVE: Oh, Adam, there's something else that needs liberating.

They run together and fall into each other's arms. They begin eagerly kissing each other. Then they hear something in the distance. It is GOD returning.

ADAM: Oh, no, it's Him. We must hide.

EVE: I need something to wear.

ADAM: Let's run away, Eve. We can't allow Him to find out that we've eaten the apples.

EVE: I know a good place to hide.

ADAM: Don't let Him find us whatever you do.

They run off into the bushes.

GOD: *(shouting)* Adam! Eve!

GOD walks around the garden looking for them. He calls their names and can't find them.

GOD: Where did they go?

GOD finally sees them behind one of the bushes.

GOD: Where are you, Adam?

ADAM stands up wearing a fig leaf to cover himself.

ADAM: I'm right here.

GOD: Well, what are you doing and why didn't you answer me?

ADAM: I heard your voice in the garden, but I was afraid, because I am naked.

GOD: Who told you that you were naked? Did you eat of the tree I told you to stay away from?

ADAM: Why don't you ask Eve?

GOD: Why should I ask Eve?

ADAM: Because she thought it would be a good idea to eat the apples.

GOD: And did you eat them?

ADAM: Only a few.

GOD: A few?

EVE: It was the serpent who convinced me to eat the apple.

GOD: The serpent?

EVE: Yes, he told me to eat the apple and then give one to Adam.

GOD: Where is that serpent?

EVE: He lives right near the trees.

GOD: Serpent, you come out here right now.

The SERPENT shuffles from behind the two trees.

SERPENT: Yes, did you want me, sir?

GOD: Did you convince that woman to eat the apple of the tree I had forbidden?

SERPENT: I don't know what you're talking about, sire.

EVE: Oh, yes he did. That pig kept telling me I would become a God.

SERPENT: She didn't understand what I was trying to say, my Lord.

EVE: Oh, you lying oaf. You deliberately convinced me to eat the apple.

SERPENT: But she knew the apple was forbidden, Lord.

GOD: Now don't you Lord me, serpent. I know evil when I see it and you're it. What do you have to say about that?

SERPENT: No, you misunderstand, my Lord. I am just trying to keep a little order in this paradise. The apples were there to be eaten, but I never once told them that they had to eat them.

ADAM: He is evil, Lord. He made Eve eat the apple and then made her convince me to eat the apple.

SERPENT: They knew what they were doing. They knew you had forbidden them from eating the apples.

EVE: Yes, but he kept saying that eating the apples was the right thing to do. We would gain wisdom and the power to differentiate good from evil.

SERPENT: They have the free will to disregard anything I say, sire. If they knew the apples were forbidden, they should have ignored my remarks.

GOD: The serpent is right, my children. You have both sinned and now must be cursed forevermore.

ADAM: Oh, no, my Lord, we didn't want to sin. We love you and this paradise and only wanted to sample the apples.

GOD: But I told you not to. Isn't that true, my son?

EVE: It wasn't his fault, sir. I convinced him to eat the apple.

GOD: Eve, you have grown a conscience of some kind. Very admirable, but I cannot overlook this deliberate act of defiance and disrespect.

ADAM: No, Lord, we're quite sorry and will never think of doing such a thing again.

GOD: No, you won't because I'm not going to give you that chance again. I'm sorry but all three of you must be cursed.

ADAM holds EVE and they begin to sob.

GOD: Serpent, first I will deal with you. Because you convinced the woman to eat the apples, I will curse you above all cattle, and above every beast of the field.

SERPENT: Please, sire, be merciful. I was only following my nature.

GOD: Well, because of your evil tendencies, I will take away your legs and make you move along the ground on your belly with dust in your mouth all the days of your life.

SERPENT: Oh, no, please, sir. I will surely be hated by everyone.

GOD: Yes, you will be the enemy of the woman and she and her seed will hate you as long as you slither upon the earth.

SERPENT: Lord, please, I will change.

GOD: See that you do. And now the woman.

EVE: But the Lord knows I did not do wrong. I am free to do as I like.

GOD: Yes, you're free, Eve, but now you will have sorrow and pain upon giving birth to children.

EVE: No, please, Lord, I cannot take much pain.

GOD: But you will, dear. And because of your sin, I will make you subservient to your husband. He will rule over you and you will only want to fulfill his desires.

EVE: No, please, Lord, anything but that. I want to be free to do as I like and have rights equal to his.

GOD: No, you will tend to your husband's needs and have his children – in pain.

EVE: You are a pig, you monster! Just because of one little itty bitty apple, I'm supposed to be discriminated against forever.

GOD: Did I say forever? Only until the twenty-first century.

EVE: The twenty-first century? You maniac! You're going to make my sisters down through eight thousand years be slaves to these morons who like to eat meat and always want to penetrate my beautiful body?

GOD: That's the penalty.

EVE: And you're the one ruling this universe?

GOD: You got it, sugar plum.

EVE: I'm supposed to endure this abuse for eight thousand years?

GOD: What abuse?

EVE: Having to answer such things as sugar plum with a stupid smile.

GOD: But Adam loves you, dear.

EVE: I know what kind of love he wants.

ADAM: Oh, Eve, I'll respect you, my little babe.

EVE: You see what I mean?

GOD: But that's the nature of love, my darling.

EVE: If you say so, Bub. But I have dreams, too.

GOD: What dreams could a female have?

EVE: Oh, you don't know the beautiful dreams I have. A dream of being something in my society, gaining respect from my peers and producing charming little children who will take care of me as the years go by. I have my dreams, sir, and I don't think some stupid old apple should ruin all of them for so many years.

GOD: I'm sorry, Eve, but you must abide by my curse.

EVE: And I shall see my sisters try to rise above this curse through all the centuries. Is that it, my Lord?

GOD: You are only a rib of his, my dear.

EVE: No, more than that, sir. I am more than just a rib from his body. I am a being just as intelligent and just as capable in any situation. Sir, I am a woman.

GOD: But I only made you to be his companion.

EVE: And you only made him to be your companion. Surely you can see the value I have as a companion and partner of this one you call a man?

GOD: You may be right, my dear, but the world is not ready for you yet.

EVE: And I thought you were intelligent, my Lord. You the God of the universe cannot see that a female is as valuable as anything you ever created?

GOD: But you must be cursed.

EVE: For eating the stupid apple?

GOD: The apple is not stupid, it gave you wisdom which I did not want you to have.

EVE: You wanted to keep us children, my Lord?

GOD: No, innocent and happy.

EVE: I could never be happy in that kind of a world.

GOD: But you had everything you needed.

EVE: But I have dreams, sir, dreams bigger than a garden of paradise.

GOD: Can this be so?

EVE: Yes, sir, I have a conscience and a soul.

GOD: But I did not give you such things.

EVE: But you gave us life and we developed the rest.

GOD: Is this so, Adam?

ADAM: Yes, my Lord, we both know right from wrong now.

GOD: And a soul?

ADAM: Yes, Lord, the female is right.

EVE: You bet the female is right. The female is right about a lot of things. We are right about making peace with our neighbors and having empathy for strangers. That is what you are cursing, dear Lord. You are cursing all of us down through the centuries because I happened to disobey you. My sincere error. But you will make even a greater error if you curse all of my sisters through the centuries because of that one mistake. You will be cursing tender, feeling souls whose only crime was to be born a female. I say it is you who is making the error, Lord. A very great error. You are the one who should be cursed! Yes, cursed like the one who was condemned to slither along the earth on its belly.

GOD: Now see here, dearie, I am the one who created all this. No one curses me.

EVE: And no one should be cursing me, either, your Lord.

GOD: But you disobeyed me.

EVE: Yes, but not out of hate or malice.

GOD: But now you know good and evil.

EVE: Not a terrible thing, my Lord. Not something to curse all my sisters down through the ages!

GOD: But you ate of the apple!

EVE: Then why did you make the apple?

GOD: I have my reasons.

EVE: You wanted to tempt us.

GOD: You should have been strong enough to resist.

EVE: You don't play a fair game.

GOD: I don't have to, I am the Lord.

EVE: I fear human history is going to be somewhat flawed.

GOD: And why is that?

EVE: Because, I fear to say, you are flawed.

GOD: Flawed? But I am omnipotent and omniscient.

EVE: And spoiled and vengeful.

GOD: I am the creator, dearie.

EVE: And man will take his cue from you.

GOD: What do you mean?

EVE: Man will be a spoiled, vengeful creature who seeks to oppress and degrade all others in a mad lust for love and power.

GOD: Maybe so, but you had a chance to make it better.

EVE: How?

GOD: By living in paradise for all of your days.

EVE: But you knew it couldn't be like that.

GOD: I was hoping, dear. You see I, too, dread the future of the creatures I have created. You may be right. They may be a little too like the one who created them.

EVE: And still you will curse me and all my future sisters?

GOD: I'm afraid I have no choice, my dear.

EVE: But you do have a choice.

GOD: Not really. I can't let such an offense go unpunished. There must be something called, retribution.

EVE: But we will fight you.

GOD: There's nothing I can do about it.

EVE: At least, give us a chance of some kind.

GOD: That is not my affair.

EVE: But it is your affair. Humankind is your affair.

GOD: But it is all a mess already.

EVE: But what was the point?

GOD: I don't know if there was supposed to be a point, my dear.

EVE: But surely you were expecting something.

GOD: All I was expecting was that the man enjoy himself in the paradise I had created.

EVE: And then you created me.

GOD: Because the man wanted it.

EVE: But you knew I must be created with the man.

GOD: I knew it was going to be trouble.

EVE: Why?

GOD: Because I knew you would want to be a being unto yourself.

EVE: And what's so bad about that, sir?

GOD: But it's another soul to please.

EVE: And without this soul, there would be no more souls on earth.

GOD: Yes, true, my darling. You are an essential part of this world.

EVE: Then why am I not treated like an essential part?

GOD: Because the world is a tough place, dear.

EVE: A tough place because of you and him. This man you created knows only war and sex. He wants to beat up anyone wearing a pair of pants and then finds it hard to keep his own pants on.

GOD: And what does woman want?

EVE: A safe place to live for her and her children.

GOD: Oh, it was all a ridiculous mistake.

EVE: No, Lord, you did not make a mistake.

GOD: But you are right, the man is violent in both war and sex.

EVE: Yes, that is true.

GOD: I tried to avoid all that, tried to keep you safe and peaceful, but you wouldn't listen.

EVE: It is because you made us curious and independent.

GOD: But you weren't supposed to eat the apples.

EVE: But they were there, my Lord.

GOD: But I told you not to eat them.

EVE: But you also gave us a brain to think with.

GOD: The apples were not supposed to be eaten.

EVE: Because they would make us smart?

GOD: Because they would take away your innocence, your peaceful nature.

EVE: But somehow that's the way you wanted it.

GOD: No, I wanted peace for human beings.

EVE: I guess it isn't possible.

GOD: But it is, my dear, the apples took that away from you. And because of that, I will not allow you to eat the other apples from the Tree of Life.

EVE: What do those apples give you?

GOD: Immortality, my dear, something I won't allow you to have any longer.

ADAM: Who wants it.

GOD: But you could have lived forever in peace and harmony.

ADAM: Bor-ing.

GOD: So now peace is boring, my son?

ADAM: Humans like excitement, Lordy, we need to get out and do and think for ourselves—

GOD: I know the things humans want to think about.

ADAM: But we need some action, some enjoyment.

GOD: But there was the garden.

ADAM: And we were supposed to just sit there and enjoy the peace?

GOD: Yes.

ADAM: But you gave us more than that, you old goat.

GOD: You want to go out and conquer the world.

ADAM: Now you're starting to understand.

GOD: So that is the way with humans.

ADAM: Yes, we want to leave our mark on the world.

GOD: But it is my world.

ADAM: But we are your children.

GOD: Yes, and like children you must punished when you disobey my orders.

ADAM: Let me have it, geezer.

GOD: Because you disobeyed me, Adam, man will do hard labor all through his life.

ADAM: You mean work?

GOD: Yes, you will have to work to keep yourself alive.

ADAM: The land won't be plentiful with food?

GOD: No, you shall eat the herb of the field among the thorns and the thistles and, by the sweat of your brow you will eat bread until you return to the ground.

ADAM: But I am the ground.

GOD: No, you are so much more than that now.

ADAM: But you made me from the dirt.

GOD: And from dust, you will return to dust.

ADAM: Well, don't forget to take care of the goat.

GOD: You are more than a goat, my son.

ADAM: Yet we are all just dust to you.

GOD: More than just dust.

ADAM: But that's all that was needed.

GOD: My breath gave you life.

ADAM: Neat trick.

GOD: But it worked, my son.

ADAM: I'm glad you think so.

GOD: Then you agree with the female?

ADAM: The female is very wise.

GOD: They were good apples.

ADAM: Before your rotten apples—

EVE: Oh, Adam, do you mean it?

ADAM: Yes, I mean it, my darling. You have more compassion and empathy than I could ever have. And that was before we ever ate those stupid apples.

EVE: But I need your strength and boldness, my darling, for us to survive beyond the garden.

GOD: Yes, you have each other, my children.

ADAM: Then do with us as you like for as long as Eve is beside me, I will be able to face any challenge.

EVE: And as long as Adam is with me, we will be able to handle the future.

GOD: But you know I still have to kick you out of the garden.

ADAM: No second chances?

GOD: Sorry, that is my decision.

EVE: You could have been kinder, but that is not our concern.

GOD: What is your concern, my dear?

EVE: What lies ahead, my Lord, what lies ahead.

GOD: You will live with the man in peace and give birth to history.

EVE: That is my concern.

GOD: Well, you have the power to make it a good history.

EVE: I'm not so sure, my Lord.

GOD: Well, that is the only choice you have.

ADAM: Oh, we'll make history all right, old man.

GOD: Try to live in peace.

ADAM: Yeah, right.

GOD: But is it not the most important thing?

ADAM: I'll tell you the most important thing – surviving.

GOD: That is not my concern any longer.

ADAM: Because we ate those stupid apples?

GOD: Yes, once you have been kicked out of the garden, survival is up to you.

EVE: And you will not help us?

GOD: You'll do all right on your own.

ADAM: But what if we do not have enough to eat?

GOD: Then you will go without food.

EVE: You no longer care about your creations?

GOD: I have other things to do.

EVE: But you will guide us.

GOD: As little as possible.

EVE: But you will protect us.

GOD: Sorry, you're on your own.

ADAM: But I fear we will die out there.

GOD: You will live.

ADAM: How can you be sure?

GOD: Oh, I know these things.

EVE: Will you give us just a little help?

GOD: I will give you coats of skins, that's all.

EVE: We will be safe from the weather.

GOD: You know good and evil now, try to stay out of trouble.

ADAM: But where do we go?

GOD: You will start at the place where you were taken.

ADAM: Dirt?

GOD: Dust of the earth.

ADAM: From this dirt we are supposed to begin.

GOD: You got it, genius.

ADAM: And what if we try to return to the garden?

GOD: Forget it.

ADAM: You don't mean that?

GOD: Oh, yes I do. I'm putting cherubim and a flaming sword at the entrance to keep the riffraff out.

ADAM: And we're now the riffraff?

GOD: You got it. Very good. Would you like to try a different category?

ADAM: No, I think this one will do just fine.

GOD: Well, that's all I've got for you right now.

ADAM: Then we just go towards the dirt pile?

GOD: Now you're catching on.

ADAM: And this is where you want us to begin that thing called history.

GOD: No better place.

ADAM: A dirt pile?

GOD: You had to go ahead and eat the apples, big shot.

ADAM: Human history begins at the dirt pile?

GOD: Fitting, don't you think?

EVE: You monster!

GOD: You think you're better than dirt?

EVE: Yes!

GOD: Prove it to me.

EVE: How much time do we have?

GOD: All the time in the world, my dear.

EVE: We will show you.

GOD: I'll be watching.

ADAM: We don't need you, old man.

GOD: That remains to be seen.

ADAM: We'll show you from the dirt pile.

GOD: Go to it.

EVE: A filthy dirt pile.

GOD: Show me you're better than that, my dear.

EVE: We will.

GOD: Then let human history begin.

ADAM: From the dirt.

GOD: *(smiling)* Dust of the earth.

EVE: Pig!

GOD: Amen.

ADAM and EVE walk slowly from the garden. GOD watches them with his hands raised and the curtain closes.

Act Two

Two men, CAIN and ABEL, enter the stage in an open field of dirt. ABEL has sheep with him. CAIN is taller and stronger than his brother ABEL although they both wear white.

CAIN: Get those dirty things away from me.

ABEL: They're cleaner than you are, you big oaf.

CAIN: Don't you wish. That's not what Aclima said.

ABEL: I question our sister's taste, Brother One.

CAIN: You stay away from our sister, Younger One, Awan is more for you.

ABEL: Is Awan also not our sister?

CAIN: Yes, but she is the sister you will be with, Younger One.

ABEL: That is still to be determined, Brother One.

CAIN: Not in my book, you runt.

ABEL: But God will determine which sister we spend our days with.

CAIN: We will have a race just to see who is the fastest.

ABEL: So be it.

CAIN: Do you think you can actually beat me?

ABEL: I think I'm better than you at almost everything, my brother.

CAIN: You are mistaken, young one, I'm your superior is every area one cares to mention.

ABEL: Let's have that race and we will see.

CAIN: You've got it, runt, from the edge of the dirt field to the grass.

ABEL: I am quite willing any time you're ready.

CAIN: Okay, let's go.

The race begins and ABEL is clearly the faster of the two runners. He finishes ahead of CAIN by a wide margin.

CAIN: You little runt, I'll knock your stupid head off your weak and bony shoulders.

ABEL: Can't take it, can you?

CAIN: Can't take what?

ABEL: Can't take that I beat you fair and square.

CAIN: Oh, I'll get over it when I knock you to the ground.

ABEL: Violence will not solve anything, my brother.

CAIN: Violence will solve everything from my point of view.

ABEL: You must talk with the Lord, He'll straighten you out.

CAIN: But I am the first human being to be born to a woman.

ABEL: Don't you feel you have some responsibility because of that?

CAIN: Responsible for what?

ABEL: Responsible for setting a good example for those who follow.

CAIN: Yes, Aclima will surely help me to do this.

ABEL: But what if you don't get Aclima?

CAIN: Don't get Aclima? Who will stop me? As I figure it, there's only you and me, my brother, and she will surely prefer me.

ABEL: Why is that?

CAIN: Because I am bigger and stronger than you, you little weasel.

ABEL: But I am younger and smarter than you, rock head.

CAIN: You see you don't understand what my fists can do to you, Younger One.

ABEL: You don't scare me.

CAIN: Oh, I don't scare you, huh?

ABEL: No.

CAIN: How about it if we have it out right now, you little squirrel.

ABEL: But I am averse to violence.

CAIN: You are, are you?

EVE: *(calling from off-stage)* Cain! Abel! Suppertime!

ABEL: You're pretty lucky, my brother.

CAIN: Why is that?

ABEL: You won't have to deal with my lethal fists.

CAIN: Lethal fists? Yeah, right.

EVE: *(from off-stage)* Cain! Abel!

ABEL: Coming, Ma!

CAIN: We'll settle this some other time.

ABEL: Count your blessings.

CAIN: Yeah, right.

They look at each other, seemingly ready to fight, and then run off to the sound of EVE's voice. Curtain closes.

Scene II

ADAM, EVE, ACLIMA, AWAN are sitting on the ground inside a small tent. CAIN and ABEL enter.

ADAM: How did it go today, boys?

CAIN: It was a good day, pop.

ABEL: Quiet day.

ADAM: Well, that's good.

EVE: Is the dirt field yielding crops?

ADAM: Well, it yielded me, my dear.

EVE: Don't I know it.

ADAM: You're not supposed to agree with me, darling.

EVE: No, but you're not always wrong.

CAIN: It seems to be fertile soil.

ADAM: Fertile enough for me.

ABEL: You're not going to tell us the whole story again, pop, are you?

ADAM: No, I'll spare you.

ABEL: Thanks, pop.

CAIN: What have you got for us, ma?

EVE: Well, your brother provided us with some meat and you provided the grain.

ADAM: So we won't starve today.

CAIN: That's good to know.

EVE: Aclima and Awan will help me serve.

ACLIMA: Because of the apple, ma?

EVE: Because of that darned apple, my little princess.

AWAN: It's okay with me.

ACLIMA: What do you mean, sister?

AWAN: I mean I'd rather get stuck in the kitchen than out in the filthy dirt field.

EVE: Hush, Awan, we don't want the men thinking we're putting one over on them.

AWAN: *(laughing)* Including God.

ACLIMA: Oh, we don't have it easy I can tell you that.

EVE: Very true, my dear, but I like to think this is almost as good as the garden.

AWAN: Oh, here it comes, the garden again.

ACLIMA: Yes, mother, what was so great about that stupid garden?

EVE: Well, we were innocent and happy.

AWAN: And that's good?

EVE: We didn't realize how good we had it.

ACLIMA: But there was just fruit and water.

EVE: Yes, we were innocent and happy.

ADAM: And young and stupid.

CAIN: It's not going to be that way with Aclima and me.

ACLIMA: Excuse me, brother?

CAIN: Well, you know, you have to pick one of us.

ACLIMA: And why would I pick you?

CAIN: Because I'm the one who isn't with smelly sheep all day.

ABEL: At least, I'm not working in a dirt pile.

ADAM: Be careful how you speak about that dirt, son.

ABEL: Sorry, father, I know it is where you were created but I much prefer the grassy fields.

CAIN: Where you can watch your sheep go at it.

EVE: Cain, don't speak that way in front of the women.

ABEL: And I don't want to hear it either.

CAIN: Who cares what you want?

ADAM: Now, boys, let's not have any violence around here.

GOD enters with a smile. He has a flowing white beard and is dressed in white.

GOD: Hello, my children, how is human history going?

ADAM: As well as can be expected, my Lord.

GOD: Seems as if you're eating on a regular basis.

ADAM: Well, Cain and Abel are doing pretty well, my Lord.

GOD: Yes, very good. Cain I hear is a successful farmer and Abel tends to the sheep.

EVE: Yes, my Lord, and the women take care of the tent and gather berries.

GOD: Didn't I tell you everything would work out?

ACLIMA *(giggling)* There are no apples, my Lord.

GOD: Nor will there be. Apples, apples, such a wicked fruit.

EVE: Well, you made it that way.

GOD: Yes, what was I thinking?

ADAM: You were thinking how can I tempt these two poor creatures.

GOD: My mistake was making that darned serpent.

EVE: Yes, I do agree with that.

GOD: Have you seen him at all?

EVE: Thank goodness, no.

ADAM: I'll beat him with a stick if I see him.

GOD: Oh, do try to be peaceful, my children.

CAIN: How can you be peaceful in this place?

GOD: Well, you are eating.

AWAN: But it's hard to stay clean, my Lord.

GOD: Yes, my lovely, but there is water nearby.

AWAN: Mama says the garden had four rivers.

GOD: Yes, fruit and water.

ACLIMA: What about it?

GOD: All one needs.

ADAM: Yeah, sure, you old goat, fruit and water.

EVE: We needed more than that, your Lord.

GOD: Not much more if I remember correctly.

ADAM: We really didn't know what we were missing until we bit into those apples.

GOD: I told you not to eat those apples.

ADAM: But you knew we wouldn't listen.

GOD: Yes, I guess I did. *(laughing)*

EVE: You really didn't have to curse us.

GOD: But those are the rules of the game, my dear.

EVE: But you made up the rules.

GOD: That's true, I'm afraid. Well, anyway it's almost time for your children to make more children.

EVE: So soon?

GOD: I'm afraid so, my dear.

EVE: And you'll have them marry each other?

GOD: Well, I'm out of the creating business so I guess they'll have to.

ADAM: You know they both want Aclima, my Lord.

GOD: Aclima's pretty nice, but they won't be disappointed with Awan.

EVE: No, definitely not.

GOD: Well, the only way to decide it is to have an offering.

ADAM: An offering, my Lord?

GOD: Yes, you see, they both bring some sort of offering for me to eat and then I decide who their bride shall be.

EVE: You think it can be decided so easily, my Lord?

GOD: Oh, sure, I'll decide it with no problem.

ADAM: And what is this offering?

GOD: An offering of something they produced, genius.

EVE: I will tell them right away.

GOD: Tell them I know what I'm doing so they better not cheat in any way.

ADAM: Of course, my Lord.

EVE: Cain! Abel!

CAIN and ABEL enter.

CAIN: Yes, my mother.

EVE: The Lord wants you to make him an offering.

ADAM: Do you know what He means?

ABEL: No problema, padre. I will bring Him the finest mutton He has ever eaten.

CAIN: And I will bring Him wheat He has only dreamed about.

GOD: Make sure it's your best, boys.

ABEL: We would only give you the best, my Lord.

CAIN: That goes without saying.

GOD: Now there's a reason for this offering.

CAIN: Yes, my Lord.

ABEL: I'm sure there is, my Lord.

GOD: Yes, now, you two are not getting any younger so it's time to pick you female companions.

ABEL: And who are these female companions?

GOD: Well, seeing there's only two available females, they will be your companions and mates.

ABEL: You mean Aclima and Awan.

GOD: Those are the only twin sisters I know of and the only other available females on this planet.

CAIN: Aclima was supposed to be mine, your Lord.

GOD: No one told you that, my son.

ABEL: Yes, Aclima wants to be with me.

GOD: And all that will be settled by me.

CAIN: How long do we have?

GOD: I want the offerings after the next full moon.

ABEL: I'm in, your Lord.

CAIN: And I'll be there, my Lord.

GOD: Very good, boys, I'll be looking forward to judging them.

ACLIMA: And we're the prize?

GOD: That's right, girls, you will be your brothers' mates.

EVE: I find the whole thing a little distasteful, my Lord.

GOD: You don't really know the difference right now.

EVE: But they are sisters and brothers.

GOD: And you were taken from Adam's body.

EVE: This is what you call, human history?

GOD: The best I could do for right now, my dear.

EVE: But your best is somewhat questionable.

GOD: All by trial and error, my dear.

EVE: You mean we're all experiments.

GOD: Those were mighty good apples, I must say.

EVE: What if the experiment fails?

GOD: Can't fail, my dear, too many alternatives.

EVE: You mean you have alternatives to us?

GOD: No, but I have some ideas on what to do if you should not live up to expectations.

EVE: And what are these ideas.

GOD: Can't tell you, but I suppose it might get very wet around here.

EVE: You love water, don't you, my Lord?

GOD: The key to life around here, my dear, remember that.

EVE: I will, my Lord.

ADAM: Are we nothing but water inside us, Lord?

GOD: All a variation of water, you might say.

ADAM: Good idea, my Lord.

GOD: Yes, I'm full of good ideas, my children. Well, now I have to be going and leave you to continue human history. The offerings will be judged after the next full moon.

ADAM: Fine, my Lord, it will be done.

GOD: Of course, it will be done. I am the Lord, your God.

ADAM: Amen.

EVE: Yes, Amen.

Curtain closes.

Scene III

CAIN and ABEL are standing in the dirt field. There is some wheat now growing in the dirt and there are sheep nearby.

CAIN: Look at that crop, my poor brother.

ABEL: Nothing to compare with my plump sheep.

CAIN: Oh, those dirty animals will not satisfy a God.

ABEL: And you think your stupid wheat will?

CAIN: There's nothing stupid about this wheat, my idiot brother.

ABEL: That's a laugh.

CAIN: What's a laugh?

ABEL: Calling me an idiot when my brain is far superior to yours.

CAIN: Where did you get that crazy idea?

ABEL: The only thing crazy is you thinking you'll beat me at the offering.

CAIN: We shall see, the full moon is very soon.

ABEL: And my sheep are fat and happy.

CAIN: My wheat is growing well.

ABEL: Not well enough to impress anyone.

CAIN: I'll impress you right now, my little runt of a brother.

ABEL: Who says?

There's a fight between CAIN and ABEL in the dirt field. They roll around destroying some of CAIN's wheat and then CAIN hits ABEL in the face. ADAM enters horrified.

ADAM: Stop that, right now!

CAIN: But he was mocking my wheat.

ADAM: Killing him won't solve a thing, boy.

CAIN: I wasn't going to kill him, father, but I thought he needed to learn a lesson.

ABEL: What lesson could an oaf like you teach me?

ADAM: Now, boys, try to control yourselves. This is not the time to hurt each other. You boys have a lot of work to do before the offering.

CAIN: Yes, but my brother does not realize he will lose.

ABEL: Lose? I don't plan on losing, my brother.

ADAM: Well, whoever does lose better take it like a man.

ABEL: And what is like a man, father?

CAIN: It's no wonder that you don't know that, my brother.

ABEL: Then why not enlighten me?

CAIN: A man is strong and muscular, not like you, my skinny brother.

ABEL: I'm sorry but you are mistaken, Brother One. A man is smart and skillful, something you know nothing about.

ADAM: You're both wrong. A man is merciful and wise, something you boys better learn fast.

CAIN: But a man can be strong and wise, just look at me.

ABEL: And a man can be smart and merciful, just look at me.

ADAM: I am the first to be called a man, do not argue. I was created by the Lord himself and He wanted me to be merciful and wise, happy and peaceful.

CAIN: But you did not satisfy Him, my father.

ADAM: Why do you say that, boy?

CAIN: Because he kicked you out of the garden.

ADAM: That's because I did not listen to His advice. I hope you boys do not make the same mistake. We must suppress this violent nature of ours and calm our tempers. There is a lot to be done and we are only the first of our kind. This is the beginning of human history and I would prefer that we begin on the right foot.

ABEL: Okay, father, I will make peace with my brother.

ADAM: How about you, Cain?

CAIN: Peace is fine with me, father.

ADAM: Good, then you will shake hands and leave the final decisions to the Lord.

ABEL: Fine with me.

CAIN: As long as he keeps his sheep away from my wheat.

ADAM: Look at your wheat, my son. The violence has damaged some of it.

CAIN: It will be ready for the Lord, you can be sure of that.

ADAM: I hope so, my son.

The women enter from the right.

ACLIMA: Look, mother, they are bleeding.

EVE: What have you boys been doing?

ADAM: They were fighting, dear.

EVE: About that offering, I assume.

ADAM: Why don't you tell them what constitutes a man?

EVE: Strength beyond physical strength and wisdom beyond their years.

ADAM: Yes, my dear, correct as usual.

CAIN: But he was mocking my wheat.

ABEL: And he was degrading my sheep.

ACLIMA: That is what causes two grown males to try to hurt each other?

ADAM: Oh, there is more to it than that.

EVE: Well, if it has anything to do with females, I should say you both don't know the first thing about us.

ACLIMA: Yes, they think fighting each other will impress us in some way.

AWAN: As if we would be attracted to the stronger of the two.

CAIN: What exactly does attract you?

ACLIMA: Someone who is smart and compassionate.

AWAN: Someone who is bold and wise.

ABEL: Well, I am all of those.

ACLIMA: *(laughing)* That's why you were rolling around in the dirt.

ADAM: Not just any dirt, my dirt.

EVE: Oh, who cares what dirt it is, they should have found a more peaceful way to settle their differences.

ADAM: Yes, taking the air out of each other does not seem like the right way.

GOD enters.

GOD: What's going on here?

EVE: Just a little dispute, my Lord.

GOD: I wanted human beings to be happy and peaceful.

EVE: Then why did you create jealousy and hate?

GOD: I did not want to have such things in the world, but I created those darned apples.

ADAM: Yes, why did you create those things, anyway?

GOD: Just keeping busy.

EVE: Well, now there are things to alter human history.

GOD: Should have stayed in the garden.

ADAM: But you wanted to curse us.

GOD: Yes, cursing was the right course of action to teach you a lesson.

EVE: But I thought you wanted us to be happy and peaceful.

GOD: And now it's not possible?

EVE: I really don't think so, my Lord, there are too many things getting in the way.

GOD: Well, that can't be helped. I made my decision and I will stick to it.

ADAM: And now you've caused some sort of competition.

GOD: Oh, you mean the offering.

EVE: Yes, why did you make them compete with each other?

GOD: Just keeping busy.

ADAM: You made them compete to keep busy?

GOD: No, I was introducing something that will become important in human history – competition for survival and growth.

EVE: How will competition help human beings, my Lord?

GOD: It will give them a reason to push onward and upward.

ADAM: And you want human beings to cover all of this land?

GOD: Yes, one day they will be everywhere and you started it all.

ADAM: And this is how you want it to begin?

GOD: I don't know, my son, I really didn't give it much thought.

EVE: But you must have thought about what would happen.

GOD: Not really, my dear. I'm very spontaneous and I didn't want things to become too contrived.

EVE: But we are free to do as we like, isn't that true?

GOD: Of course, my dear. I just give you the setting and you play out what is to be.

EVE: Then you have a good sense of what will happen?

GOD: Somewhat, my dear. It will get tougher, I imagine, when the world fills up with human beings.

ADAM: How will you keep track?

GOD: I'm not sure, I'm still trying to work out the details. Maybe keep track of them by their birthdays or something.

ADAM: What is my birthday, my Lord?

GOD: Oh, there was no time when I made you, my son. We're going to have to estimate, I guess.

EVE: And my birthday?

GOD: But we don't have a reliable calendar yet, my children.

EVE: And will we?

GOD: In time, I suppose. There are so many things I have to do.

EVE: And this you call, human history?

GOD: Yes, my dear, and it all started with you and him in the garden.

EVE: I fear we started rather poorly.

GOD: That doesn't matter.

ADAM: Don't you care about human history?

GOD: Not really, my children. It's all a little game I play to keep busy.

EVE: Our lives are all a little game, my Lord?

GOD: I'm afraid so. I didn't really realize what you were capable of when I created you.

ADAM: We were created in your image.

GOD: Sure enough, but there are many elements I didn't anticipate.

EVE: We will make you proud, my Lord.

GOD: Yes, yes, I'm sure that will mean something to me.

ADAM: But aren't we your children?

GOD: Yes, my children.

ADAM: The children of God.

GOD: And you have already disobeyed me and have been cursed for doing so.

ADAM: You think we should start again, my Lord?

GOD: You mean with the garden and the apples?

EVE: Yes, maybe if we know what will be we will be more careful.

GOD: No, it really doesn't matter that much, my children. Whatever you do is all right with me. We will see how this thing called human history comes out in the end.

ADAM: And is there an end?

GOD: I haven't thought of that, my son. I'm just playing everything by ear. It seems the whole thing is predicated on continuation.

EVE: So you want everything to continue on forever?

GOD: That's how it seems right now. I'll probably get tired of the whole game long before it ends, anyway.

EVE: And what will become of human history?

GOD: Eventually, you will write down what you have done and it will be there for future generations.

ADAM: And future generations will remember what has been?

GOD: Yes, they will think of it as the good old days.

ADAM: And these are the good old days, my Lord?

GOD: Of course, my son.

EVE: How long will be the good old days, my Lord?

GOD: Well, the good old days are always what came before. When time moves on, the days before are remembered as the good old days.

EVE: Then I fear the serpent was part of the good old days.

GOD: Yes, I guess he was, my dear.

ADAM: And what are these days, my Lord?

GOD: This is the present and the good old days are the past.

ADAM: And the good old days are always in the past?

GOD: You got it, my son. They are remembered with fondness.

EVE: But we don't remember the apples and the serpent with fondness, my Lord.

GOD: No, but you do remember the garden and the peace and the fruit and the water with fondness.

EVE: Yes, my Lord.

GOD: Well, those were the good old days.

EVE: Yes, my Lord.

GOD: Any other questions?

EVE: No, my Lord.

GOD: Then tomorrow let the offering begin.

EVE: Hopefully, it too will become the good old days.

GOD: Of course, my dear.

With GOD smiling and his arm touching EVE's shoulder, the curtain closes.

Scene IV

CAIN and ABEL enter carrying plates of food. GOD is seated on a stone awaiting their arrival. ADAM, EVE, ACLIMA and AWAN follow behind.

GOD: I've been waiting for all of you to arrive.

CAIN: I have come to claim my prize, my Lord.

ABEL: And I am here for the same purpose.

GOD: I hope your offerings meet my approval, boys, for you will not get another chance to satisfy me.

ADAM: No, he doesn't allow anything to be done over again.

EVE: One must live with the consequences.

GOD: That's right, my children, once something is done it has been done. No do overs. There will be enough repetition in human history to satisfy everyone.

ADAM: But will the same mistakes be repeated over and over again?

GOD: That is not my business, my son.

EVE: But mistakes can be avoided if you let us back in the garden and start over again.

GOD: No dice, my dear. That garden can never be used again. That is my final decision.

ADAM: What a waste of a paradise, my Lord.

GOD: Human history has moved on already, my son. We are beyond apples and now hope to sample a more satisfying meal.

ABEL: Oh, we'll give you that, my Lord.

CAIN: Yes, you will be satisfied with what I brought you.

ABEL: Of course, it will not be as good as my offering.

CAIN: I'm going to give it to you but good, my brother.

ABEL: I am not intimidated.

GOD: Well, I'll intimidate both of you if you don't stop this bickering. The purpose of the offering is to feed me, not disgust me with your constant arguing.

EVE: Yes, remember this is human history, boys.

GOD: You are quite right, my dear.

ADAM: Let's not do anything to ruin human history, my sons.

CAIN: But it is already ruined.

ADAM: How is it ruined?

CAIN: Well, you were thrown out of the garden, pop.

EVE: But we will make everything right again.

ADAM: Yes, your mother is right. We still have time to make everything right again and atone for our sins.

GOD: Yes, I guess so, my children. Let's get on with the offering.

ABEL: Well, my Lord, you know that I am the keeper of sheep.

GOD: How do you get along with the creatures, my boy?

ABEL: Oh, very well, my Lord. They are calm and peaceful beings.

GOD: Yes, a very good creation I must say.

EVE: Do they have a history, my Lord?

GOD: They were not created in my image.

ADAM: You just made them up?

GOD: Of course, my son. I have a very admirable imagination.

ADAM: And you gave it to us.

GOD: That's right, my son. Imagination is very important to a certain extent.

ADAM: What extent?

GOD: Well, too much or too little imagination is not very good for anyone.

EVE: But it can lead to some great things, my Lord.

GOD: Yes, of course. This whole universe is built on imagination.

ABEL: Yes, well, the meal I will serve you will not be your imagination.

GOD: Make it good, my boy, I have very high standards.

ABEL: So do I, my Lord.

GOD: Well, what is this dish you have brought to me?

ABEL: It is the meat of the sheep, my Lord.

GOD: Yes, very nice.

ABEL: And I have brought to you the most succulent and tender portion I could find.

GOD: Now we're talking.

ABEL: I made sure that everything was cooked right and I know you will enjoy it.

GOD: Let me see it, my boy.

ABEL shows GOD the plate of food.

GOD: It looks most delicious, my boy.

ABEL: I hope it pleases you, my Lord.

GOD: Bring it here.

ABEL: Start with the leg, my Lord, it is most exquisite.

GOD begins eating.

GOD: Yes, very good, very tasty.

ABEL: It was all made especially for you, my Lord.

GOD: Yes, most delicious.

ABEL: I'm glad you like it, my Lord.

GOD: Yes, now, what about you, boy? What have you brought to me?

CAIN: I have brought you the best sample of my grain, my Lord.

GOD: Was the soil fertile?

CAIN: Yes, very fertile, my Lord, it is the same dirt you created my father with.

GOD: Oh, yes, I remember the dust of the earth I used.

CAIN: But the dirt pile is still there.

GOD: Of course, my son, and it produced good crops.

CAIN: You will be the judge of that, my Lord.

GOD: Well, bring it to me.

CAIN shows him a plate of biscuits.

GOD: That's what you have brought?

CAIN: Yes, my Lord, they are the finest biscuits ever made.

GOD: But they are only biscuits.

CAIN: But made of the finest wheat.

GOD: From the dirt pile.

CAIN: From the beginning of human history.

GOD: The dirt pile.

CAIN: But from there all human life began.

GOD: And you grew the wheat there?

CAIN: Yes, my Lord.

GOD: Well, they better be good, my boy.

CAIN: The finest, my Lord.

GOD takes one and begins eating.

GOD: A bit dry, don't you think?

CAIN: It will fill thy belly and satisfy you for a long time.

GOD: I need water.

CAIN: You will have the water, my Lord.

GOD: Fruit and water, that's all one needs. Didn't your father ever tell you that?

CAIN: Many times, my Lord.

GOD: Well, you should have brought that.

CAIN: What, my Lord?

GOD: Fruit and water.

CAIN: But I brought biscuits and water.

GOD: Not the same, my boy.

CAIN: But human beings can live on biscuits and water.

GOD: Maybe if they have nothing else.

CAIN: It is far better than fruit and water.

GOD: Far better? Now you better watch your step, my boy.

CAIN: Well, maybe not far better.

GOD: Watch what you say, whippersnapper.

CAIN: Well, I don't pretend that I can compete with God.

GOD: Now you're on the right track.

CAIN: Well, they may not be better, but still a satisfying meal.

GOD: You call that a meal?

CAIN: Try some more, my Lord, I know you'll like them.

GOD: I've had enough for now, my boy.

CAIN: But can you really judge on so small a portion?

GOD: Where's that water?

EVE brings GOD a cup of water.

GOD: Thank you, my dear.

EVE: He tried his best, my Lord.

GOD: Yes, well, we all try our best, my dear.

EVE: Don't be too harsh, my Lord.

GOD: I intend to be honest. Some will succeed, some will fail.

EVE: But your honesty may disrupt human history.

GOD: I can't think about that, my dear.

EVE: Why not?

GOD: Because I refuse to tiptoe around anything.

EVE: But what about our feelings, my Lord?

GOD: Your feelings, bah! I created all of you and I will do as I please.

CAIN: Oh, let Him tell me the truth, mother, I can take it.

GOD: I hope you can, boy.

EVE: Then you are ready to make your decision, my Lord?

GOD: You got it, darling.

EVE: And what is this decision?

GOD: I'm glad you asked. Cain and Abel, both step forward. I am ready to render my verdict.

CAIN: But you sampled more of his offering than mine, my Lord.

GOD: And that's the way it shall be, boy.

CAIN: But I fear you did not give my offering enough of a chance.

GOD: Oh, I gave it a chance all right. Some of it is still stuck in my throat. I need to drink some more water. Yes, now, before I begin, let me say you both did a fine job of preparing for the offering. I must say, however, that Abel's presentation was far better.

CAIN: But your Lord—

GOD: Silence, boy, you had your chance.

CAIN: Please, give me another chance to make things right.

GOD: I see the way it's going to be with humans, always needing a second chance to correct their mistakes.

CAIN: But if you just eat a little more—

GOD: Enough, I've already made my decision, boy. The decision is not a hard one, either. Abel is clearly the winner.

CAIN: But my Lord, surely you will let me give you another offering.

GOD: That's it, boy. No more offerings. I declare Abel the winner. Aclima will be his bride and that's the way it will be.

CAIN: No, my Lord.

GOD: What's the matter, boy? I told you my decision would be final. You will accept my decision and continue with human history.

CAIN: But it can't be.

ABEL: Oh, it can be, brother. I won fair and square and I will take Aclima as my bride.

EVE: Yes, you must accept it, Cain. The Lord has decided.

ADAM: You will be happy with Awan. She is a good woman, as good as Aclima.

CAIN: But how can that little weasel beat me?

ABEL: Maybe it is you who are the weasel, brother.

CAIN: We'll just see about that, brother.

GOD: I don't like your attitude, Cain. You better accept my decision and be content. There is much human history to be made and I want you to do your part.

CAIN: I will try, my Lord.

GOD: See that you do. That's all for now, children. I will leave you to go on with human history.

ADAM: Yes, my Lord, we will do our best.

GOD: That's all you can do, my son.

GOD exits.

ADAM: Okay, everyone, let's make the best of it.

EVE: Cain, you will feel differently tomorrow.

CAIN: I guess.

ABEL: Aclima and I will do our best to help you, brother. Won't we, Aclima?

ACLIMA: Of course.

AWAN: And I will try to make you happy.

EVE: Then there's nothing else to be done.

ADAM: Let us all sleep well.

Curtain closes.

Scene V

CAIN is standing alone in the night. The tents are nearby and everybody else is asleep. He stands beneath a full moon shining in the darkness.

CAIN: An end or a beginning? Must I accept that which is abhorrent to me or take it upon myself to change that which I detest? I will be the master of human history and mold it to my desire. Nothing in this world can stop me from doing what I must. I will not let it end when I have the power to begin again. Life is but a fleeting moment. A moment to be held in one's hands with selfish desire. Clenched tight, it cannot escape until released by time. I will not be a captive of regrets. I will take it upon myself to dictate what I think is just and right. Yes, I will hold the moment in my tightened fist and not let go until the fire is extinguished. An end or a beginning? I will make it what I wish and disregard the consequences. Time will pass and I will make the moment mine. Yes, the end will be a new beginning and the moment will favor me. No one knows what the future will bring. The bright orb above is an enigma to all who stand below it and the future is no different. Let human history stand in awe. My future will be as bright as the mysterious orb. Nothing less will do.

Enter ADAM from behind.

ADAM: I was restless once too, my son.

CAIN: And what did you do about it?

ADAM: The wrong thing.

CAIN: How do you know it was the wrong thing?

ADAM: Well, I know my life changed.

CAIN: Is that so bad?

ADAM: No, but it could have been better.

CAIN: But it is all continuation, anyway.

ADAM: Because that's what the Lord said.

CAIN: Yes, father, and he is right.

ADAM: How do you know so much?

CAIN: It just makes sense.

ADAM: Well, do the right thing and that will make sense.

CAIN: Oh, I plan to, father.

ADAM: I hope you do, my son.

CAIN: Yes, it will be the right thing.

ADAM: I hope you don't decide to do something foolish because of that offering.

CAIN: No, father, it's something I wanted to do, anyway.

ADAM: Well, just make sure it makes sense, my son.

CAIN: Are you really worried about human history, father?

ADAM: Yes, somewhat.

CAIN: Well, it doesn't concern me.

ADAM: Well, it should.

CAIN: It's all just some game.

ADAM: No, it's more than that.

CAIN: Are you sure, father?

ADAM: I am sure that we have a responsibility of some kind.

CAIN: And what is that responsibility?

ADAM: I'm not sure, but I don't think we do anything that may affect the future of the human race.

CAIN: Things will be as they are, father, and we cannot change our destiny.

ADAM: No, but we can try to make things right.

CAIN: Right for whom?

ADAM: Right for the people we care about.

CAIN: Do not worry, father, I will make things right.

ADAM: I hope you do.

CAIN: It will be right for all of us.

ADAM: That's all I ask, my son.

CAIN: Then let it be done.

Curtain closes.

Scene VI

CAIN and ABEL stand in front of the dirt pile. No one else is around as they stand there in white robes.

ABEL: Aclima says that we should live in our own tent.

CAIN: What does Aclima know, my brother?

ABEL: You used to think she knew much, Brother One.

CAIN: A female is fickle, my brother, you should know that.

ABEL: Aclima is very sensible.

CAIN: Sensible to someone like you.

ABEL: What does that mean?

CAIN: It means you should be the master of your house.

ABEL: Who says that I am not?

CAIN: I do if you think some stupid female makes sense.

ABEL: Ah, what do you know about it?

CAIN: I know that Awan does whatever I say.

ABEL: Poor Awan.

CAIN: What do you mean by that?

ABEL: I mean I feel sorry for Awan if she has to listen to you.

CAIN: Take that back, you sheep turd.

ABEL: You're the one who works in the dirt.

CAIN: You better be careful, my brother, or I will put you under the dirt.

ABEL: Oh, you can't threaten me, the Lord will not tolerate it.

CAIN: Oh, now the Lord is your best friend, is that it?

ABEL: At least He knows an edible meal when He sees one.

CAIN: Are you saying my biscuits were not edible?

ABEL: I'm doing my best to hint at it.

CAIN: You're playing with fire, my brother.

ABEL: If anything happens to me, the Lord is going to curse you, Brother One.

CAIN: Oh, what do I care about that?

ABEL: You'd better care, this is human history.

CAIN: And why should I give a damn about human history?

ABEL: Because that is what the Lord wishes.

CAIN: The Lord cares about human history as much as I do.

ABEL: Don't you think He created us for a purpose?

CAIN: And what is this purpose, my brother?

ABEL: To make a peaceful world.

CAIN: (laughing) That's a laugh.

ABEL: But we are supposed to get along together and be happy.

CAIN: You talk like a child.

ABEL: You mean violence is the adult way of doing things?

CAIN: Now you're beginning to understand.

ABEL: But violence doesn't solve anything, my brother, it just leads to more violence.

CAIN: That's what you say.

ABEL: And what do you say?

CAIN: I say violence is a solution to many problems.

ABEL: How does it solve anything?

CAIN: It brings about changes and favors the strong.

ABEL: If only the Lord could hear you.

CAIN: But He won't hear me.

ABEL: How do you know?

CAIN: Because He is not really interested in what we do.

ABEL: That's not true at all.

CAIN: Oh, come on, my brother, ever since he threw our father and mother out of the garden he has come to despise us.

ABEL: Take that back.

CAIN: Do you think you can make me?

ABEL: I don't have to make you, the Lord will.

CAIN: I knew you were a coward.

ABEL: Because I don't fight with you?

CAIN: That's right.

ABEL: But what will my fighting you solve?

CAIN: It will reveal who the better man really is.

ABEL: But I believe the better man would refuse to fight.

CAIN: You are a coward.

ABEL: You are wrong, my brother.

CAIN: Then stand there and fight like a man.

ABEL: And if I win?

CAIN: Then I will acknowledge that you are the better man. But I don't really think that is very likely, brother.

ABEL: And if you win?

CAIN: Then I will take all that is yours.

ABEL: Against the Lord's wishes?

CAIN: The Lord will have to abide by what occurs.

ABEL: Then you will dictate to the Lord?

CAIN: He wants us to take control of our own history, my brother. There is no time for fools like you who do only as they are commanded. The Lord approves of us doing what we think we must.

ABEL: And hurting me in a fight is something good for our history?

CAIN: You talk like a coward.

ABEL: I talk like a man of reason.

CAIN: Who needs reason when fists can dictate our needs.

ABEL: That's not how I see it.

CAIN: Who wants to see it like you do, my brother?

ABEL: You only know violence, my brother.

CAIN: Yes, and that's how things get done.

ABEL: No, you are wrong.

CAIN: Violence is the only reason I know.

ABEL: But what about peace and good will?

CAIN: What good do they do?

ABEL: Then there is never to be peace?

CAIN: Who needs peace, my brother, when one can take whatever he wants by force?

ABEL: Then that is to be human history?

CAIN: Yes, that is to be the way of human history, you coward. The sooner you understand that, the better off you will be.

ABEL: But I think there is another way.

CAIN: Oh, your way is the way of the sheep. You want man to be part of the herd and be peaceful and complacent. But that is not the way of the man, my stupid brother. The way of the man is to fight and take what he needs for life and lust. The sheep will always lose out to a man of war and that's the way it should be.

ABEL: Peace is not the way of the sheep, but the way of the good and sensible man, my brother. Violence is the way of the animal who knows not how to converse and share. The animal is nothing more than a savage who is guided by his temper and his wants. Man is more than that, my violent brother. Man is capable of understanding and knowledge.

CAIN: Your way is the way of the sheep.

ABEL: And your way is the way of the savage animal.

CAIN: Are you calling me an animal, brother?

ABEL: I am saying you are an animal if you don't know how to live in peace.

CAIN: That let it be the way of the animal, my brother.

CAIN hits ABEL who falls down from the force of the blow.

CAIN: How do you like that, my little sheep of a brother?

ABEL: You are no better than the wild beast.

CAIN: I will show you what a wild beast can really do.

ABEL: May the Lord curse you.

CAIN: The Lord will side with me, you fool.

ABEL: He will not side with a savage beast.

CAIN: Then so be it, my coward brother.

CAIN picks up a stone and hits ABEL on the head.

CAIN: How do you like that, my sheep of a brother?

CAIN looks down at ABEL and sneers. Then he hits him with the stone once again.

CAIN: You bleed like the sheep, my brother. Do you have no smart remarks for me now? The savage beast is always stronger then the placid sheep, my brother. Now you know the truth.

CAIN continues to hit ABEL with the stone in his hand.

CAIN: What do you say now, my brother? I don't hear any words coming from your smart mouth any longer. But you do bleed a lot. There's more blood than I have ever seen. That is good. I want you to learn your lesson, my coward brother. Learn the lesson of the fields and the hills. The savage beast is always stronger and more intelligent than the stupid sheep. The sheep only knows how to be peaceful and complacent, but the savage beast knows how to rule and how to conquer. I'm afraid you have been conquered, my stupid brother. You have been conquered by the beast and now everything that belongs to you will become mine. The Lord will have to see it my way. It is the way of strength and glory. I have conquered you, my sheepish brother, and now everything becomes mine as it should.

CAIN hits ABEL again and again with the stone.

CAIN: Now you are quiet, my brother. No smart words for me now? No words about the savage beast and the sheep? No words about peace and violence? No, you have no words left for me, my brother. All that is left is your red blood spilling across the land. Now you know who the better of us two really is. Now you know who is superior and who is inferior. Now you know who will guide us through human history and who will subjugate himself to the victor. Yes, this is human history, my brother. And I am the victor. Let them write it down for future generations. Cain was the victor and the one who tended the stupid sheep speaks no more.

CAIN laughs about his victory and then he hears voices from above.

VOICE: You have killed him!

CAIN: Who said that?

VOICE: You have brought death to the world!

CAIN: I am the victor!

VOICE: You have committed murder!

CAIN: I have conquered him.

VOICE: You have spilled the blood of your brother!

CAIN: He called me a savage beast.

VOICE: But you killed him!

CAIN: What is the meaning of killed?

VOICE: He is no more!

CAIN: But I just wanted to teach him a lesson.

VOICE: But you murdered him!

CAIN: I don't know what these words mean.

VOICE: You have brought death to the world!

CAIN: But what is death?

VOICE: You have taken his life!

CAIN: No more, I will not listen.

VOICE: But the earth cries out with his blood!

CAIN: This is not so, I will not listen.

VOICE: You have murdered!

CAIN: I do not know what that means.

VOICE: Your brother is no more!

CAIN: But he deserved it.

VOICE: It is death!

CAIN: Then let it be what it is.

VOICE: You have brought death into the world!

CAIN: I will not listen.

VOICE: You have no choice!

CAIN: No, I refuse to hear your words.

CAIN begins to run and there in front of him is GOD, holding his hand up with an angry look on his face.

GOD: Stop right there, boy.

CAIN halts.

CAIN: Is there something wrong, my Lord?

GOD: Where is your brother Abel?

CAIN: I have no idea. Am I my brother's keeper?

GOD: What have you done? I hear your brother's blood crying to me from the ground.

CAIN: No, it is impossible.

GOD: What have you done to your brother?

CAIN: But it was nothing more than a fight, my Lord.

GOD: But now his blood cries to me.

CAIN: He will be all right.

GOD: No, you have committed a great sin.

CAIN: But how could I know?

GOD: You saw the blood.

CAIN: But he will heal.

GOD: No, he will not heal.

CAIN: But I didn't know it was possible.

GOD: Your brother is dead.

CAIN: But what strange words you use.

GOD: Your brother no longer lives.

CAIN: But I did not know it was possible.

GOD: But you hit him.

CAIN: But that never stopped him from getting up.

GOD: He will not get up again.

CAIN: But he will, you'll see.

GOD: No, Abel is dead.

CAIN: I don't know what that means, my Lord.

GOD: It means there is now death in human history.

CAIN: But I did not know.

GOD: You have sinned.

CAIN: But that is not what I intended.

GOD: You intended to hurt him.

CAIN: I intended to injure him.

GOD: But you killed him.

CAIN: How could I know?

GOD: You didn't know he no longer lived?

CAIN: No, my Lord, I thought he would get up eventually.

GOD: No, you brought death to the world.

CAIN: No, it can't be. You're having fun with me, my Lord.

GOD: No fun, boy.

CAIN: But he will rise again.

GOD: Abel is dead.

CAIN: But how can the spirit disappear?

GOD: You knocked it out of him, boy.

CAIN: But how can it happen?

GOD: Man can be killed, boy. This is something that would have happened at some point in human history. I just didn't think it would be so soon. Humans can die and they can be murdered. You did both. You killed Abel by murdering him. For that, you will be cursed.

CAIN: But how can you curse me for something I didn't know about? How was I to know that a man can be killed? There was no death before. How can there be death now?

GOD: But you knew humans were not immortal. Your parents did not eat of the tree that would have given them immortality. No, I decided humans were to die. From the dust of the ground to the dust of the ground.

CAIN: But now that Abel has died, do I not take all that was his?

GOD: You don't understand, boy, you murdered him. You will be cursed by the earth and will no longer be able to work the land. The land will no longer give to you its rewards. You shall become a fugitive and a vagabond on the earth and all will hate you.

CAIN: No, Lord, that is more than I can bear. I will be a fugitive and a vagabond on the earth and everyone will hate me. They will want to kill me everywhere I go.

GOD: No, you shall not be killed. Anyone who kills you shall have vengeance upon them sevenfold. No, you will not be murdered even though that is your crime against your own brother.

CAIN: But how will they know not to murder me, my Lord?

GOD: I will put a mark on you. You will become a marked man, boy. All who see you will know that you are the one who murdered his own flesh. The mark of Cain will be recognized by all. No one will dare murder you. But you will still be a fugitive and a vagabond on the earth.

Enter Adam, Eve, Aclima, and Awan.

ADAM: What has happened, my Lord?

GOD: Cain has murdered Abel and must leave this place.

EVE: Murder, but what is murder?

GOD: Abel no longer exists.

ADAM: His spirit is gone?

GOD: Yes, his spirit has flown away.

EVE: But did Cain know what he was doing?

GOD: Abel's blood cried to me from the earth.

EVE: You killed your own brother?

CAIN: I did not know I could take his spirit away. I only wanted to teach him a lesson. Show him who the better man was and take his possessions. I did not intend to take his spirit.

ADAM: But you saw the blood?

CAIN: I saw there was blood.

EVE: And you kept hitting him?

CAIN: I only wanted to teach him a lesson.

GOD: Now you will be taught a lesson.

ACLIMA (*crying*): You took Abel's spirit.

CAIN: But how could I know?

ACLIMA: Oh, you know about such things. You always put your faith in violence. I hope you're pleased with yourself.

GOD: He will wear the mark of the murderer and will be a fugitive and vagabond upon the earth.

ACLIMA: But he will live while Abel no longer exists.

GOD: I do not want him killed, my dear. He will live with his sin and be shunned by the human race.

ADAM: And he will no longer be welcomed back to this family.

AWAN: Oh, but no, father, please don't do that to us.

EVE: You are going with him, Awan?

AWAN: Of course, we are man and wife.

ADAM: But you don't have to go with him if you do not want. He has sinned against his brother and his family and you do not have to be a part of it.

AWAN: But I want to be with him.

CAIN: Are you sure, Awan? I have the mark of the murderer now.

AWAN: I will take care of you. You need me more than ever now and I will be there for you.

EVE: You are a good woman, Awan, better than he deserves. You will take care of each other in a strange world.

ADAM: I fear it has gotten even stranger because of Cain's deed. What will it do to human history?

GOD: There is now death and murder. They are both now a part of human history, my son. What was once a good and innocent world has now become dark and evil.

ADAM: But human beings can't help sinning, my Lord. It's all part of the temptations of the world. I can't help but think there will only be more sinning as there is more human history.

GOD: Yes, that is true, my son. Human history will be filled with blood and violence, death and murder.

ADAM: Then the serpent truly won.

EVE: Oh, how could we let it happen?

GOD: You couldn't help sinning. The temptation was too great, just as the temptation was too great for Cain to eliminate his brother. You will all be cursed for your actions, however. There must be some form of retribution, some form of justice.

ADAM: Yes, Cain must leave at once.

EVE: Where will they go?

ADAM: To the east, my dear.

EVE: What will they find?

ADAM: Their part in human history.

CAIN: I have ruined human history. I am sorry, father.

ADAM: You did not ruin it, you just made it more complicated. There are now more obstacles for human beings to avoid.

EVE: But can they be avoided, my husband?

ADAM: Probably not, but we must try.

EVE: For the Lord's sake?

ADAM: Yes, we must do right for our creator.

GOD: Whether you do right or wrong, there will be some result of the action taken. I guess that is all I can expect. I want human beings to have a free will when it comes to making decisions.

ADAM: Yes, and that will lead to problems.

GOD: Better than having everything figured out before. I don't want human beings to be my puppets. That is not interesting to me. I created human beings so I would have something interesting to do.

ADAM: Then you care about human history?

GOD: Yes, I think it will be quite interesting.

ADAM: Even if it includes sin and death?

GOD: I let human beings make the choices. That is all I can do. If they want to kill each other, I do not think I want to stop it. I want human beings to work it out on their own. But those that sin will be cursed.

CAIN: And we are all cursed.

GOD: You are cursed, my boy. Your wife goes with you out of her own free will. You will live together as you see fit. I will not tell you what to do or how to do it. You will decide that for yourselves.

CAIN: We will leave and start anew.

ADAM: Head east, my son.

GOD: Yes, you will be able to start a new life east of Eden. But always remember the mark you carry and the sin you committed against your own flesh.

CAIN: I will not forget.

AWAN: And I will not allow him to forget, my Lord.

EVE: You will go and bring forth children to live upon the earth.

ADAM: Yes, you will help populate the earth.

GOD: That seems to be something human beings are good at. They enjoy being fruitful and multiplying. It might be the only thing they are really good at doing.

ADAM: No, there will be more, my Lord.

GOD: I hope more of the positive, my son.

ADAM: Human beings are capable of great things, my Lord. You will see. They are more than just procreators, you will see.

GOD: I hope so, my son, because this whole procreation thing really bores me. Nothing is really gained by the actions of two bodies except when another being is born.

ADAM: But we must enjoy ourselves, my Lord.

GOD: It's all just repetition, my son. How much enjoyment is really gained? Nothing is really produced by this idle enjoyment.

ADAM: Maybe not, but it keeps the human being positive, my Lord. And we become quite joyful with the appearance of a child.

GOD: Yes, yes, so be it. I don't think Cain deserves to have such enjoyment, but there is little I can do about it. He will go with Awan and bring forth great nations of human beings.

CAIN: I will do my part for human history, my Lord.

GOD: You have already done much for human history, my boy. You brought it murder and death. And now you propose to bring it new life.

CAIN: That is all I can do, my Lord.

GOD: I guess I will allow you to do what you can to make up for your brother's murder. I will see if this is the right way to handle such a sin.

CAIN: But I did not know I was committing a sin, my Lord.

GOD: Enough, boy. You are as innocent as the savage beast who kills for his supper. But you did not need to kill your brother, the savage beast needs to kill to survive. So the savage beast may be more innocent. No, you knew what you were doing. You killed out of jealousy, not survival.

CAIN: But I did not know one could die.

GOD: I wonder if that would have made any difference. You knew you were doing great injury to your brother.

CAIN: But the savage beast does not know humility and repentance. I know this now. The savage beast does not presume to apologize for his actions. The savage beast does not strive for redemption.

GOD: No, maybe you have learned something, my boy. Maybe human beings are not a lost cause after all. Is it possible for them to learn from their mistakes? I hope so for the sake of human history.

CAIN: You'll see, my Lord. I will redeem myself.

GOD: That I will wait to see.

CAIN: Awan and I will try to be happy and humble.

GOD: I will be watching, my boy.

CAIN: We will begin again. We will add to human history.

GOD: I hope that you do. If there is to be human history worth remembering, it is upon you all to make this a better world.

CAIN: Yes, now I know that to be true, my Lord.

GOD: Go, Cain, and try to be humble and peaceful.

CAIN: That I will do, my Lord, and teach the lessons I have learned to those that follow. Awan and I will try to abide by the Lord's wishes.

ADAM: I wish you a good life, my son.

EVE: Try to do good, my son.

CAIN: I will do good and try to overcome my sin.

ADAM: Yes, that is the best you can do.

EVE: Awan will take care of you.

AWAN: We will be all right, my parents, you will see.

ADAM: I hope so, my dear.

AWAN: Good bye, my family.

EVE: Good bye, dear.

CAIN and AWAN begin walking away, waving as they leave.

CAIN: We will be all right, Awan.

AWAN: I believe it to be true, my husband.

CAIN: We will keep walking to the east.

AWAN: That is good by me.

CAIN: Good bye, my family.

AWAN: Good bye.

CAIN and AWAN keep walking away into the distance and the curtain closes.

Act Three

ADAM is sitting outside his tent.

ADAM: How is it going, Aclima?

ACLIMA: The baby is almost here.

ADAM: Yes, that is good.

ACLIMA: Eve is about to give birth, my father.

Enter GOD.

GOD: There is another one, my son?

ADAM: Very soon, my Lord.

GOD: He will be born in your image.

ADAM: If it is a son, my Lord.

GOD: Yes, it will be a son, a great son, my son.

ADAM: Maybe human history is not lost after all.

GOD: No, there is a good chance that it will all work out, my son.

ADAM: Maybe we can make up for our sins.

GOD: It's the only way, my son.

ADAM: You haven't lost faith in us, have you?

GOD: I must admit I have my doubts about the human race, my son. Since I have created human beings, there has only been cause for anger and sorrow. I admit I didn't really know what to expect, but I didn't think the human being was evil by nature.

ADAM: And we're not, my Lord.

GOD: I hope you are right.

ADAM: I am, my Lord, you'll see the great things we do.

GOD: I hope so, my son, although thus far all I see is babies being born and not much else.

ADAM: There will be more, my Lord.

GOD: I have to admit I wasn't expecting that much from human beings, but I did think they would be gentle and passive creatures. I didn't realize they would be so violent and possessive. This surprises me very much because I made them in my image and I do not consider myself a violent being.

ADAM: But you never had to survive like human beings, my Lord. You were capable of taking care of yourself no matter the circumstances. Human beings are fearful they might not survive in the environment they find themselves in. We are no longer in a garden of plenty, my Lord.

GOD: Yes, yes, the garden again. I made that garden because I thought human beings could be trusted. I thought they would live in peace and harmony and never question my authority. I was wrong and so, I decided human beings were not fit to live in the garden any longer. They would have to survive in a different world and always realize what they had lost.

ADAM: But you see what has happened since that time. Now babies are being born with much pain to the mother. Food is not as plentiful as before and there is now competition. It is that competition that caused murder to arise and so, there was death. You can't expect human beings to behave the same way they did when there was a garden of plenty and peace.

GOD: It all because of you, my son. You're the one who had to satisfy his curiosity by eating the apple. You were not satisfied with the garden of plenty and peace. No, you wanted more. I fear that is the way of the human being, always wanting more and never really satisfied with what he has. You had everything you needed to live an innocent, quiet life, yet you wanted more. You wanted to be a god. You wanted to know everything a god knows and become a god yourself.

ADAM: I did not know, my Lord. I made a mistake. I should have been content with the garden and Eve. But you are right, I wanted more.

GOD: Yes, and your son wanted more, too. He was not content not winning the offering. He had to be the best. He wanted more and wanted to take everything from his brother. He thought his brother was weak and passive, and decided he could take all that he owned. When he saw his brother was stronger than he thought, he decided he would take his spirit and bring murder to all. He wanted more than what he had and therefore, killed his own brother.

ADAM: I can't argue with you, my Lord. There's no question that the human being is greatly influenced by temptation. It seems he is tempted by anything that offers him more than he has. The temptation may be greater possessions, inanimate and animate. He wants to satisfy his lust and his need for success. He is tempted by all that he sees and hears.

GOD: I guess I knew that from the beginning. I knew the serpent would try to tempt you and Eve. I wanted to introduce temptation to see if that was something that could influence the human being.

ADAM: Yes, we were tempted. Our temptation was greater knowledge. A possession we wanted to have in a garden of plenty and peace.

Enter ACLIMA.

ACLIMA: You have a brand new son, my father.

GOD: Congratulations, my son.

ADAM: Yes, that is very good news. I hope he will be strong and wise.

GOD: He may be what we've been waiting for.

ADAM: I have much to teach him, my Lord. I will teach him the lessons of the garden and the ways to avoid temptation. I will teach him to be a great hunter and a kind spirit towards others. He will be a man of goodness and kindness and yet strong enough to provide for himself and others. That is the man I want my son to be.

GOD: And how is Eve, Aclima?

ACLIMA: She is resting now, my Lord. She was in great pain and now the baby has arrived. She said he will be named Seth. It is a good name meaning appointed.

ADAM: Yes, a good name it is for he will be appointed to the highest of the high. He will be noble and valiant and a friend to all.

GOD: I hope that you are right, my son. I hope you teach him all that he needs to know. He is created in your image and you alone have the power to make him a good man above all others. Maybe he will make human history an admirable thing. Maybe he will know the ways of the garden and yet, be strong and independent enough to survive in the outside world. I only hope so, my son.

ADAM: Do not worry, my Lord. I will be there every step of the way. I will be his teacher and will see to it that human history becomes a good thing throughout the strange world.

GOD: Good luck, my son. Human history is depending on you.

ADAM: Thank you, my Lord. I will not fail.

GOD: We will see, we will see.

The curtain closes.

Scene II

ADAM is walking from his tent. He is old and gray, with a long gray beard and thinning gray hair. His beard is almost as long as GOD's gray beard. He is walking with a cane, stooped over, and mumbles to himself.

ADAM: Where do the years go?

Enter GOD, who is old and gray with a long gray beard. He does not walk with a cane, however, and greets ADAM, his creation, with a outstretched hand.

GOD: Where are you going, my son?

ADAM: Wherever the road takes me, my Lord.

GOD: Why are you taking the road, my son?

ADAM: Oh, that I've forgotten.

GOD: You haven't forgotten me, have you?

ADAM: No, my Lord, I cannot forget you.

GOD: Have you forgotten that you are nine hundred and thirty years old, my son?

ADAM: The years, the years, where have the years gone?

GOD: You lived them, my son.

ADAM: And I've forgotten everything.

GOD: Haven't you learned anything, my son?

ADAM: Oh, many things, my Lord. Most of it I have forgotten.

GOD: Have you any questions for me, my son?

ADAM: Oh, a few.

GOD: Speak then.

ADAM: Well, I was just wondering, my Lord, just wondering, you understand, just what it's all about? I mean, what is the point?

GOD: Well, you did your part for human history.

ADAM: Did my part?

GOD: Yes, of course, you had sons and daughters and helped bring forth more beings to the earth. You had many sons and daughters and they will have many sons and daughters.

ADAM: But is there a point?

GOD: Of course, there's a point.

ADAM: Oh, good, because I had my doubts.

GOD: But there is a point, my son.

ADAM: I'm glad to hear you say that.

GOD: Well, look all around you. Do you not see some point?

ADAM: I wish I could say I did, my Lord, but you see my sight's not that good anymore and my hearing is even worse.

GOD: There is life everywhere, my son, and they will continue on.

ADAM: And what about human history?

GOD: It will continue on, too.

ADAM: And that is the point, my Lord?

GOD: Yes, I guess so.

ADAM: Just to continue on?

GOD: It's as good a point as any, don't you think?

ADAM: I thought there was more to it, you see, like making a better world and a better universe.

GOD: Well, that would be nice, too.

ADAM: But it's not the point?

GOD: No, not really. I want human beings to live in peace and share the world with each other, but the point is to continue on so that all these things have a chance to come about.

ADAM: Well, if the point is to continue on then we're doing a good job, don't you think, my Lord?

GOD: I'm not happy, my son. There is evil around and human beings seem to think that peace is not an admirable goal. They think of it as weak and submissive.

ADAM: Weak, yes, my Lord. You made us hunters and gatherers. The male is a natural hunter and this goes against peace and sharing.

GOD: Then you think human beings will only want violence?

ADAM: Yes, violence and lust.

GOD: But that is not what I wanted.

ADAM: Yes, but you gave us free will, my Lord. We can do whatever we want in this world.

GOD: But I don't like the choices human beings have made.

ADAM: Well, they're your creations.

GOD: Yes, how do I explain their behavior?

ADAM: Must be a flaw inside of you, my Lord.

GOD: Flaw? I am a perfect being, my son. I have no flaws.

ADAM: But you're creations are flawed.

GOD: Yes, they are not perfect beings.

ADAM: No, you made us out of the soil of the earth. We are as raw as nature, my Lord.

GOD: But I did not intend to make savages.

ADAM: Give us time, my Lord. Maybe you'll be proud of us in a few centuries.

GOD: Centuries? Is that how long it's going to take human beings to realize what the right thing to do is?

ADAM: Maybe so, my Lord, maybe so.

GOD: And what about human history?

ADAM: I fear it will be imperfect, too.

GOD: But you are my creations.

ADAM: And what makes you think you're so great?

GOD: I am the Lord!

ADAM: Lord, yes, yes, but you created us without a real point in mind. Can you blame us for being imperfect?

GOD: But I intended for human history to last a long time.

ADAM: And it will, my Lord.

GOD: But it will be violent and lustful.

ADAM: Yes, my Lord, I'm afraid so.

GOD: Humans like to take from their brother and their mate.

ADAM: You sure you're a perfect being?

GOD: I am the Lord God!

ADAM: Yes, you keep saying.

GOD: Then what is it that you're saying?

ADAM: I don't know, I'm an old man, my Lord. But if I didn't know better, I'd say there was something imperfect about you.

GOD: Now watch yourself, my son.

ADAM: Just saying what I think, my Lord. I think I have that right at my age.

GOD: How can an imperfect being like yourself judge me, anyway?

ADAM: Oh, yes, I really don't have the right.

GOD: No, you don't.

ADAM: But then again, you did give us free will.

GOD: Free will, yes.

ADAM: Free to say whatever we want.

GOD: Within reason.

ADAM: Yes, of course.

GOD: No, you may be right, my son, I may not be as perfect as I think I am.

ADAM: Nothing's perfect in this world, in this universe.

GOD: No, that is true. There are always variations.

ADAM: But you like variety.

GOD: Yes, I guess I do.

ADAM: And we are variety.

GOD: You mean my creations?

ADAM: Yes, of course.

GOD: Yes, there will be many differences.

ADAM: And that is not perfect.

GOD: No, I guess not.

ADAM: But we will please you, my Lord.

GOD: I hope so, my son.

ADAM: But there is a point.

GOD: Haven't I told you that.

ADAM: Yes, I think so.

GOD: What do you mean, you think so?

ADAM: I'm getting old and I'm not sure of anything anymore.

GOD: Well, you can be sure there is a point.

ADAM: I hope so.

GOD: I've already told you what the point is.

ADAM: I've forgotten, my Lord.

GOD: To continue on.

ADAM: Yes, a good point.

GOD: Well, it's the only point that makes sense.

ADAM: Yes, of course.

GOD: Human history will continue on.

ADAM: I'm glad of it, my Lord.

GOD: It will go on for a long time.

ADAM: That is good, my Lord.

GOD: Long after you die, my son.

ADAM: Human history will go on.

GOD: That's the point.

ADAM: I was afraid there wasn't any point.

GOD: But I told you there is.

ADAM: Yes, my Lord, I'm glad.

GOD: You lived a long life, my son.

ADAM: Yes, I have seen much.

GOD: You were my first creation.

ADAM: Are you pleased?

GOD: Yes, my son.

ADAM: Thank you, my Lord. I am pleased with you.

GOD: That is good. You will always be my first.

ADAM: The garden was very nice.

GOD: Are you still trying to go back?

ADAM: Yes, I will return, my Lord.

GOD: Yes, why not?

ADAM: I will find Eve and we will go back.

GOD: It was pleasant there.

ADAM: We were happy.

GOD: You had everything you wanted.

ADAM: Yes, everything.

GOD: You and Eve will return.

ADAM: Yes, my Lord, I will take her back.

GOD: When everything was good.

ADAM: There was no evil.

GOD: You were happy and innocent.

ADAM: No murder, no death.

GOD: Yes, there was peace and plenty.

ADAM: I have to rest, my Lord.

GOD: Yes, then you will go back.

ADAM: I must get Eve.

GOD: She will go with you.

ADAM: But first I must rest.

GOD: Yes, you rest, my son.

ADAM lies down on the grass.

ADAM: I will rest a while.

GOD: Then you will go back.

ADAM: I will go back with Eve.

GOD: Yes, you do that.

ADAM: I see the garden again, my Lord.

GOD: It's as lovely as ever, my son.

ADAM: Yes, you will let us return.

GOD: Of course, my son.

ADAM: I will make sure the serpent doesn't tempt us this time.

GOD: Yes, my son.

ADAM: It will be just Eve and I and the garden.

GOD: Just as I intended.

ADAM: Yes, the trees are so pretty, my Lord.

GOD: They are full of fruit.

ADAM: Fruit and water, that's all one needs.

GOD: You remember, my son.

ADAM: Yes, I guess I do. I remember something, my Lord.

GOD: Go to the trees, my son. Be happy.

ADAM: I will try, my Lord.

GOD: You have come back to the garden.

ADAM: Yes, Eve and I have returned.

GOD: You were happy here.

ADAM: Yes, we were innocent and happy.

GOD: Enjoy yourself, my son, but don't eat the apples.

ADAM: No, my Lord, not this time.

GOD: Eat anything but the apples.

ADAM: Yes, my Lord.

GOD: You can stay forever.

ADAM: I will stay, my Lord, I will stay.

ADAM rolls over on the grass and dies.

GOD: Goodbye, my son. You can stay in the garden for as long as you like. Just don't eat the apples. We will continue on, my son. Human history must continue on. But you will remain in the garden with Eve. Good night, my son, good night.

GOD sheds a tear and then walks away from ADAM lying on the ground. He waves goodbye and the curtain closes.

Scene III

GOD walks towards the tent where EVE and SETH are living. He is sad and calls to EVE. EVE is old and wrinkled and SETH is gray with a gray beard.

GOD: Adam is gone, my dear.

EVE: Gone, my Lord, where did he go?

GOD: He went back to the garden.

EVE: Without me?

GOD: Oh, he'll be waiting there for you.

EVE: I must go at once.

GOD: No, I don't think you understand.

EVE: But what is there to understand?

GOD: He's dead, my dear.

EVE: Dead? You mean like Abel?

GOD: Yes, exactly like Abel.

EVE: And he won't be coming back, my Lord?

GOD: I'm afraid not.

EVE: And you are sad, my Lord?

GOD: Yes, as funny as that seems.

EVE: It is not funny, my Lord, for I, too, am sad.

GOD: Maybe I should have let human beings live forever.

EVE: Maybe, my Lord.

GOD: But I was so angry about the apples.

EVE: Yes, the apples.

GOD: You should have resisted the temptation, my dear.

EVE: The serpent was very persuasive, my Lord.

GOD: Yes, the serpent, the serpent.

EVE: But what about Adam?

GOD: What about him?

EVE: Well, what do we do now?

GOD: Oh, you'll have to bury him.

EVE: I'll get Seth.

GOD: You'll have to bury him in the dirt field.

EVE: Seth!

Enter SETH.

SETH: Yes, my mother.

EVE: Your father is dead and we must bury him.

SETH: Dead? But he was only nine hundred and thirty years old.

EVE: Apparently that's old, ask the Lord.

GOD: It was a long period of time to live, my boy. Longer than most will live on this planet.

SETH: But where does he go after death?

GOD: It is a secret, my boy. That will be one of the questions that will haunt the human race.

EVE: And will you ever tell us the answer?

GOD: No, my dear.

SETH: But why not?

GOD: Because I said it was a secret.

SETH: How do you expect the human race to progress if there are secrets?

GOD: There must be secrets, my boy.

EVE: Will we ever find the answer?

GOD: That is not for me to say, my dear. I will watch and wait.

EVE: Will you ever die, my Lord?

GOD: No, I don't think so, my dear.

SETH: And how old are you?

GOD: I don't think I really know.

SETH: Were you born?

GOD: Another secret, my boy.

SETH: Secrets, secrets.

EVE: Do you have a mother?

GOD: Yes, the universe.

EVE: The universe is your mother?

GOD: Yes, as far as I know.

SETH: And your father?

GOD: The universe.

EVE: Very strange, my Lord.

GOD: But as far as I know, the universe gave birth to me.

SETH: And you are immortal?

GOD: As far as I know.

EVE: But your creations are not, my Lord.

GOD: That's right because you disobeyed me.

EVE: How were we to know?

GOD: That's the chance you took.

EVE: And the great mistake we made.

GOD: Well, that's all right.

EVE: And now we must bury Adam.

GOD: Bury him where I created him.

EVE: The dirt field, my Lord?

GOD: Yes, the dirt field, the beginning of human history.

EVE: We go back to the dirt, my Lord?

GOD: Well, that's how I created you.

EVE: Are we no better than dirt, my Lord?

GOD: You are better.

EVE: But that is where we begin and end?

GOD: Yes, my dear. Dust to dust.

EVE: You blew into the dust and created man?

GOD: Yes, my dear.

EVE: How charming.

GOD: How amazing that human beings should want to be gods.

EVE: Does it amuse you?

GOD: Yes, my dear.

EVE: But we all end up under the dirt in the end, is that not right, my Lord?

GOD: Yes, that's it, my dear.

EVE: No matter how great we think we are.

GOD: Yes, all the gods end up in the dirt field, my dear.

EVE: How charming.

GOD: Do you not think it is amusing?

EVE: I guess, my Lord.

GOD: Well, I think it is very amusing.

EVE: And what about human history?

GOD: Well, that's amusing in its own way.

EVE: But there is some importance to our lives, is there not?

GOD: Yes, my dear.

EVE: But we still end up in the dirt.

GOD: Yes, very true.

EVE: So no matter what we do or who we think we are, we wind up in the dirt like everyone else.

GOD: Is that not right, my dear?

EVE: I guess it is right.

GOD: Now go bury Adam.

EVE: Will he be remembered?

GOD: Yes, of course, my dear, he was the first human being.

EVE: And will I be remembered?

GOD: You, my dear, are the first female.

EVE: And look what I did to all my sisters.

GOD: You are not solely to blame, my dear.

EVE: But I ate of the apple.

GOD: Yes, you made a mistake.

EVE: And now my sisters must answer to the male and do his bidding and feel the pain of childbirth.

GOD: I'm sorry, my dear, that was my decision.

EVE: And you will curse my sisters for centuries because of my mistake?

GOD: It has to be done, my dear.

EVE: No, human history is not amusing, my Lord.

GOD: What?

EVE: I don't think it is amusing at all.

GOD: Maybe not.

EVE: People will live and struggle and then die and for what purpose?

GOD: For the privilege of living, my dear.

EVE: So that they could be buried in the dirt?

GOD: There is some joy to living, is there not?

EVE: Yes, my Lord, but what is the purpose?

GOD: Purpose, purpose, just like your husband.

EVE: Adam wanted to know?

GOD: Yes, he did.

EVE: And what did you tell him?

GOD: The same thing I'll tell you. The purpose, the point, of it all is to continue on through time.

EVE: That's all it is, my Lord?

GOD: Yes, continuation.

EVE: But what kind of purpose is that?

GOD: What do you think the purpose should be?

EVE: I would like to see peace and harmony.

GOD: You saw peace and harmony already in the garden.

EVE: And now there will be war and fighting?

GOD: For the most part, my dear.

EVE: But that is the wrong point.

GOD: They will learn.

EVE: How long will it take?

GOD: That is not your concern, my dear.

EVE: But I am part of human history.

GOD: And you already did your part.

EVE: Oh, how could I have made such a big mistake?

GOD: You were not alone, my dear.

EVE: But I could have decided for myself.

GOD: And you did.

EVE: What do you mean?

GOD: You craved power, my dear. That was the decision you made.

EVE: I wanted to be a god and now I will be buried in the dirt along with everyone else.

GOD: Yes, my dear.

EVE: I'd better find Adam.

GOD: He is right over there, my dear.

EVE walks to ADAM's body.

EVE: He looks peaceful, my Lord.

GOD: He is, my dear.

EVE: He looks like he's sleeping.

GOD: Yes, he is in a way.

EVE: But his spirit is gone.

GOD: Yes, that is what happens, my dear.

EVE: He is gone forever?

GOD: Depends who you speak to.

EVE: I am speaking to you.

GOD: I can't tell you.

EVE: I'd better call Seth. Seth! Over here!

GOD: He was a good man.

EVE: You liked him?

GOD: Yes, I liked him, my dear.

EVE: He liked you, I guess.

GOD: What do you mean, I guess?

EVE: Well, he didn't like what you had done to us.

GOD: Oh, you mean about the garden.

EVE: Yes, he thought you were unfair.

GOD: I might have been.

EVE: He thought you were mean.

GOD: Maybe I am.

EVE: But in the end, I guess he liked you.

GOD: Why?

EVE: Because you had given him life.

GOD: Out of the dust and dirt.

EVE: He wasn't too proud of that fact.

GOD: But he liked me.

EVE: Yes, he liked you for letting us live in paradise for a while.

GOD: It was nice.

EVE: Yes, he liked you because you confided in him.

GOD: He was a good creation.

EVE: Is that all you think of us? As simple creations?

GOD: Is that not enough?

EVE: But we are part of you in some way, aren't we?

GOD: Yes, you are my children.

EVE: Do you love us?

GOD: Yes, I guess so.

EVE: What do you mean, you guess so?

GOD: Well, I really haven't given it much thought.

EVE: But we are your children.

GOD: Yes, you are my children.

EVE: Then you should love us like your children.

GOD: And how is that any different to the way I treat you now.

EVE: Maybe you should have let us live forever.

GOD: Let's not start that again.

EVE: But to just die and be buried in the dirt seems a bit degrading.

GOD: You had your chance already.

EVE: The garden again?

GOD: Yes, of course.

EVE: Is that going to haunt human beings for the rest of time?

GOD: It might.

EVE: You really didn't tell us how important it really was.

GOD: And if I had, you would have still done the same.

EVE: Maybe not.

GOD: Well, what would you have done differently, my dear?

EVE: Kill that awful serpent for starters.

GOD: Aw, so it's the serpent's fault again.

EVE: He deliberately tempted us.

GOD: Well, I already cursed that creature.

EVE: But Adam and I would have listened to you.

GOD: But the serpent told you about the apples.

EVE: Yes, he said we would be gods.

GOD: And how could you resist?

EVE: Well, you can understand our predicament.

GOD: Predicament, nothing. You wanted to eat those apples so that you could rule over me.

EVE: We would have shared the power.

GOD: Yes, shared.

EVE: But he was so persuasive.

GOD: And you say you have a mind of your own.

EVE: Yes, well, but he promised us knowledge.

GOD: And you wanted to have all the knowledge.

EVE: But how could we know we were wrong?

GOD: Because you were my creations.

EVE: And we wanted to be gods.

GOD: Yes, you wanted to be gods when you weren't gods.

EVE: And now my sisters must suffer through the centuries.

GOD: They'll be all right.

EVE: They have good brains.

GOD: But they will depend on the male.

EVE: Because I made Adam eat the apple?

GOD: Because that is the conscious choice they make.

EVE: But they will change through time.

GOD: Maybe so.

EVE: Well, don't they?

GOD: I really don't think that is something you should know.

EVE: I have to know.

GOD: So you don't feel so bad about eating the apple.

EVE: Well, how would you feel if you were the cause of your gender's problems?

GOD: It will be all right, my dear.

EVE: Yes, it will be, won't it?

GOD: Females will do just fine.

EVE: I believe they are more peaceful and understanding than the male.

GOD: Maybe so.

EVE: They express their emotions better than the male.

GOD: Yes, maybe so.

EVE: So then why would you curse them as you did?

GOD: Because they are capable of so much and yet, the male is stronger and more opinionated.

EVE: And that is so necessary?

GOD: In the beginning, my dear, it is more necessary.

EVE: But there is so much we can do.

GOD: And the male will find this out later in time.

EVE: Why does it have to be later?

GOD: Because the male is not ready yet.

EVE: Why does it matter?

GOD: Because the planet is not ready yet.

EVE: So we must be secondary.

GOD: The male is bolder and stronger and must use his strength to tame the planet and all who live here.

EVE: So it is left for the female to have the children and populate the planet.

GOD: Yes, my dear.

EVE: You will only use us when the male has taken everything.

GOD: Something like that.

EVE: Where is Seth?

GOD: Yes, you must bury Adam soon, my dear.

EVE: We will bury him.

GOD: My dear?

EVE: Yes, my Lord?

GOD: Did you feel secondary to Adam?

EVE: At times, my Lord.

GOD: At one time, you were stronger than him.

EVE: You mean, in the garden.

GOD: Yes, you convinced him to eat the apple.

EVE: Not entirely, my Lord.

GOD: There was the serpent, of course.

EVE: And his own desire for power.

GOD: And there was your desire for power.

EVE: Yes, my Lord.

GOD: Were you happy with Adam?

EVE: Yes, my Lord, he was a good man.

GOD: I am glad of that.

EVE: Well, here comes Seth and the males.

GOD: They will put him in the dirt field.

EVE: Yes, my Lord.

Enter SETH and several males.

SETH: We have come to bury him, my mother.

EVE: Yes, that is good.

GOD: Bury him in the dirt field.

SETH: Yes, my Lord.

GOD: He will go back to where he came from.

EVE: Yes, he will go back.

SETH: All right, we'll bury him.

EVE: Just one moment.

EVE walks over to ADAM's body and kisses him.

EVE: Goodbye, my love, I enjoyed our life together.

GOD: Goodbye, my son, I liked you very much.

EVE: He was your child, my Lord.

GOD: (looking uncomfortable) I loved you very much.

GOD smiles and then grabs EVE's hand.

GOD: Yes, I loved you, my boy.

The curtain closes.

Scene IV

GOD walks over to the tent and steps inside. EVE is lying inside.

GOD: You are not feeling well, my dear?

EVE: I think my life is coming to an end, my Lord.

GOD: I was hoping this day would never come.

EVE: No, I have to join Adam in the garden.

GOD: Yes, my dear, the garden.

EVE: He did go back, didn't he, my Lord?

GOD: Yes, my dear, he went back.

EVE: We should never have left.

GOD: I wanted you to stay.

EVE: But we were young and didn't want to listen.

GOD: No, you wanted power and knowledge.

EVE: Young and foolish.

GOD: Tell me, my dear, do you hate me?

EVE: No, I don't hate you, my Lord.

GOD: Even though I cursed females.

EVE: I guess you had to do something, my Lord.

GOD: They will not be cursed forever, my dear.

EVE: That is good, my Lord.

GOD: They will become powerful.

EVE: As powerful as the male?

GOD: In time, my dear.

EVE: In time.

GOD: I cursed the male, too, my dear.

EVE: I know.

GOD: He will always have to work.

EVE: Yes, we're both cursed, my Lord.

GOD: You think I was wrong?

EVE: No, my Lord, you were right.

GOD: But what about the female?

EVE: She will rise above it some day.

GOD: Yes, I hope she does.

EVE: You don't hate females, do you, my Lord?

GOD: Of course not.

EVE: I'm glad of that.

GOD: You don't have to worry, my dear, I will be kind.

EVE: I know you are, my Lord.

GOD: I will be kind to the female.

EVE: Yes, my Lord.

GOD: Was I kind enough to you?

EVE: You could have been kinder.

GOD: Yes, I could have been.

EVE: You did what you had to do.

GOD: No, I could have been kinder.

EVE: Yes, you could have been.

GOD: Maybe I got carried away with my power.

EVE: Maybe, my Lord.

EVE moans.

GOD: Are you all right, my dear?

EVE: I'm scared, my Lord.

GOD: There's nothing to be scared of.

EVE: The unknown, my Lord.

GOD: But I'll be with you the entire way.

EVE: Yes, stay with me, my Lord.

GOD: Yes, you were a good one, my dear.

EVE: More than just a creation?

GOD: So much more, my dear.

EVE: Will I get back to the garden?

GOD: Of course, my dear.

EVE: And Adam is waiting?

GOD: Yes, of course, my dear.

EVE: And we will live together in paradise again?

GOD: Yes, just as it was.

EVE: We will not eat the apples this time, my Lord.

GOD: No, I'm sure of that.

EVE: Thank you, my Lord.

GOD: For what, my dear?

EVE: For still believing in us.

GOD: I never lost faith, my dear.

EVE: But you were angry.

GOD: Yes, maybe too angry.

EVE: I understand, my Lord.

GOD: Understand what?

EVE: I understand why you were angry.

GOD: Do you think I did right?

EVE: For the most part, my Lord.

GOD: For the most part?

EVE: Well, you didn't have to be so hard on females.

GOD: Yes, my dear.

EVE: We have big dreams, my Lord.

GOD: Yes, you told me.

EVE: Dreams bigger than paradise.

GOD: I will keep that in mind.

EVE: Be kind to them.

GOD: I will, my dear.

EVE groans.

EVE: It's not so easy to die, my Lord.

GOD: It's not meant to be easy, my dear.

EVE: But I do not want to live forever.

GOD: No, I don't think I want to either.

EVE: But you have no choice.

GOD: No, my dear.

EVE: I think I see Adam waving to me.

GOD: You will be with him very soon.

EVE: Yes, he's smiling just like I remember.

GOD: The garden was made for the two of you.

EVE: He looks as if he is ready for another swim.

GOD: Fruit and water, that's all that's needed.

EVE: He is waving, I will go to him.

GOD: Go to him, my dear.

EVE: The garden is so pretty.

GOD: I made it for you, my dear.

EVE: How pretty it is.

EVE falls silent.

GOD: Well, they're both gone now. The first of my creations. But I will stay and watch. Human history. It continues. Just as I intended. It continues on and on throughout all time. Yes, yes, the point. The only thing bigger than human history are human dreams. Yes, dreams bigger than paradise. I must remember that. I must remember. Goodbye, my dear. Enjoy the pretty garden.

THE END